NOTES FROM BELOW

Notes from Below
Issue 23
Spring 2025

Editors
Jamie Woodcock
Callum Cant
Lydia Hughes
Wendy Liu
Sai Englert
Lorenza Monaco
Clark McAllister
Matthew
Dante Philp
George Briley
Roberto Mozzachiodi

Website
Wendy Liu

Cover design and layout
Thomas Greenwood

www.notesfrombelow.org
editors@notesfrombelow.org

ISSN 2631-9284 (Online)
Print ISBN 978-1-0683586-0-9

Notes from Below is a socialist journal written for and by workplace militants. We believe that when workers come together to fight for their own interests they don't just improve their conditions at work, but initiate a confrontation between workers and bosses that can only be finally resolved by a revolutionary transformation of society. The journal aims to actively contribute to that struggle of the working class against capitalism: an economic system that exploits us to make the rich richer and is willing to drive us toward total ecological collapse in order to do it.

We use the tools of workers' inquiry and class composition.

Workers' Inquiry is the study of work from the workers' point of view. The goal of inquiry is to understand our work better so that we can fight against our bosses and advance the wider fight against the capitalist economic system.

Class composition is a theory that allows us to analyse how the working class is organised at this specific point in time by looking at three key factors: the technical, social and political composition of the class. Technical composition is the organisation of lots of individual workers into a working class through the network of connections and relations that make up the whole economy. It is shaped by factors like how we produce value for our bosses, the technology we work with, how we are managed, and how our work fits into the work of other people. Social composition is the organisation of workers into a class outside the workplace, in our homes and communities. This is diverse and complicated, shaped by factors ranging from the kind of housing we live in, how we get to work, migration status, relationship to the state, how we buy our food, and more. Political composition is a bit different, because we shape it: it describes the ways in which we organise ourselves into a force that can take part in class struggle. It includes everything from the tactics we use in strikes, the kinds of unions we are part of, and the political parties we support (or don't). We think that when we analyse all three of these factors together, then we get a better understanding of how militant workers can intervene in wider social processes to try and accelerate the fight against a capitalist system that is based on our exploitation.

This journal focuses on work for two reasons. First, because it shapes our experience of daily life: the working class reproduces the system every day because we provide services and manufacture goods that society could not function without, and yet the system doesn't work in our interests. This experience of exploitation defines the working class viewpoint. Second, because work is the place where we have the greatest leverage over our enemies. The bosses and politicians don't care what we think, but they do care if we don't do the work that keeps reproducing the system. Work is the place where workers feel like we can turn to our boss and say "I am nothing, but I should be everything."

Want to read more on workers' inquiry and class composition? Scan the code below to read The Workers' Inquiry and Social Composition, available also in Italian, Spanish and French.

Subscribe to Notes from Below now

Notes from Below is a journal for and by workplace militants. Our publishing model is only possible because of the help of our subscribers.

Our model is simple:

£5 subscribers receive three print editions of Notes From Below a year

£10 subscribers also receive free copies of all the books we publish (or international postage for the issues.)

But the key part is that every single issue sent to a subscriber will also finance at least two free copies of Notes From Below for workers in struggle.

Ready to subscribe? Head to notesfrombelow.org/supporter or scan the code below

Contents

Editorial: Our Infrastructure and Theirs

Without our labour, nothing works. That is capitalism's dirty secret. Every day, we work to reproduce a system based on our exploitation. It happens in many different ways. We could be producing commodities that the capitalist sells for a profit, or providing services on behalf of the state, like healthcare or education. We could be raising the next generation of workers or caring for the last. It can be hard to recognise that basic fact, given all the bullshit we are surrounded by. But no matter how much they try to obscure the basic reality, we know it: *without our brain and muscle not a single wheel would turn.*

Some sections of the class, however, have a particular role to play. They work in the infrastructure of society, doing the jobs that enable everyone else to do their jobs. The systems that industries and state services rely on (energy, water, transport, communication, and so on) could be points of incredible leverage for our class. In this issue, we hear from miners, water workers, shipbuilders, tube drivers, energy workers, and militants who have supported workers' inquiries in supermarkets. This issue should be read in dialogue with pieces from our previous issues, in which workers have documented how their labour keeps society alive, from healthcare to care work. In a capitalist society, the reproduction of the working class and the reproduction of capital are two sides of the same process. There are many differences between hospitals and mines, as well as between water treatment facilities and care homes. What they all have in common is that workers can shut things down. The threat of this haunts bosses and politicians like a recurring nightmare.

We have not asked the contributors to this issue to write just because we want to understand their potential power. There are two more key reasons. First, we want to understand the strain these deep systems are under from the workers' point of view. Second, thinking about how we might reorganise these systems under workers' control is an essential task for any serious revolutionary politics.

We know, to put it simply, that shit is about to get bumpy. As we write this editorial, Los Angeles is on fire. The houses that multimillionaires sell to those other multimillionaires are burning. If they can't keep each others' mansions safe, what does that mean for the rest of us? However, this destabilisation is evident not only in spectacular disasters. It also has a more boring, everyday form. A comrade who works on the railway recently told the editors how high-speed electric trains have to turn off non-essential power use on long stretches of track to avoid overburdening the local power grid. In South East London, every few months, the water company tells people in a new area to boil their water because of a threat of contamination. Our friends who are admitted to the hospital spend 24+ hours on beds lined up in corridors. By now, we are pretty used to the idea that the ruling class has abandoned a social contract based on rising living standards. What is new is that we are now supposed to accept that the infrastructure we rely on daily, is starting to fall apart. As we argue below, the suggestion of a 'just transition' led by the state and in collaboration with capital as one way out of this perpetual decline appears all the more unworkable in these conditions.

But what does this process of deterioration look like from the inside? Is it as bad as it looks, and what are we missing about the process? How can infrastructure workers organise, and what might come next? In this issue, we hear from workers themselves so that we can learn from their privileged insights into the nuts and bolts of the infrastructures of modern capitalism.

From economic to political

As they describe in their inquiries, workers in different sectors and workplaces within infrastructure differ in their militancy. Workers are starting to find their feet in areas such as the British water industry or the Slovenian supermarket sector. On the railways, there is a tradition of workplace organisation paired with a mixed level of militancy. In practice, this has meant strike action that is strong in numbers but often limited in frequency. In some workplaces, such as the Harland and Wolff shipyards or the Soma coal mines, we have seen remarkable bursts of militancy from self-organised workforces.

Militant tactics, however, do not necessarily transfer into revolutionary politics. For example, in *When Workers Take Control,* Joe Passmore describes how the militant workforce of Harland and Wolff occupied their shipyard, demanding nationalisation by the British government and expressing aspirations of transitioning to green production. However, this action ultimately ended with a new takeover of the Belfast shipyard by another private company. Whilst undoubtedly a serious and impressive action, it did not end in a lasting experiment in workers' control. Instead, the dominant mode of production remained, and ultimately, the shipyard faced crisis again just five years later.

Like with the work-in of the Upper Clyde Shipbuilders in Scotland in 1971-72, historic moments of working-class struggle, led by shop stewards with mostly overtly socialist politics, often continue to operate within the broader logic of capital. This is not the fault of workplace militants, whose impressive feats of organisation should be applauded. Instead, it points to the fundamental difficulty of exiting an economic system whose relations have dominated for hundreds of years. As history shows, this cannot be abolished in one country, let alone one workplace. In Portugal during the Carnation Revolution, 200 industrial enterprises in many major industries came under workers' control,[1] yet this failed to materialise into a serious challenge to capitalism. Existing within a broader world market, their access to the resources needed to continue production was limited unless they continued to engage in commodity production. The social division in many workplaces under workers' control remained largely untouched. Where it was challenged, the state intervened with violence to restore it.

Yet, working-class power does not solely express itself in explosive moments of occupation and protest. As Joe outlines, referring to the 2024-25 takeover of Harland and Wolff by Spanish company Navantia, a latent desire for workers' control remained after:

> If we'd gotten bad news recently, then we would have blockaded those gates again... We will always have a way in. And when one door closes, we will always find another one.

Once these tactics have been used, they become part of the arsenal of class struggle. For example, in *Under London*, James describes how workers on the London Tube push for elements of workers' control on a daily basis. They discuss the scheduling "mafia", a group of elected reps that write the work timetables. When workers are not happy with these elected reps, they either recall them or set up a competing mafia to overrule them. However, the most visible tactic on the Tube is the strike. Through this, they aim not only to shut down their own workplace, but other workplaces throughout the capital. This tactic has won many gains for Tube workers, although it has proven less industrially effective at achieving the RMT's stated wider aim of "working for the supersession of the capitalist system by a socialistic order of society".[2]

---

1   Phil Mailer (2012) *The Impossible Revolution*. London: PM Press.

2   RMT Rule Book, Rule 4b.

Workers' control and the 'Just Transition'

The issue of workers' control comes to the fore in many of the pieces. However, a strategic bind also emerges. How can fighting for workers' control go beyond the bounds of the capitalist organisation of work? The contradictions that play out when capital is challenged but not superseded become apparent when we look at the demand for a just transition. The demand has animated attempts to win substantial progressive reform and tangible action on climate change.

Climate breakdown is no longer a threat. It is happening in our infrastructure, workplaces, and communities. This is why the promise of a Just Transition and a Green New Deal are so attractive. On an emotional level, they offered a way out. They are premised on the idea that someone else will solve our problems "from above." But there is no just transition. It is not happening - and as long as we live under capitalist social relations, it will never happen. That is the blunt reality that the inquiries in this issue point towards. Inquiry can help us to confront the actual material conditions that surround us - no matter how uncomfortable they may be.

In *Direniş means resistance,* we hear about how workers on the edges of Europe are struggling to establish elementary collective bargaining against an authoritarian state-company-yellow union 'triangle.' For them, a just transition would require defeating the state's energy policy, eliminating fractions of capital that have merged with the ruling AKP party, and challenging the dominant institutions of the labour movement. This kind of victory is hard to imagine outside of a revolutionary situation. In *When Workers' Take Control,* we hear that ambitions for retooling production around green projects have been raised by militant workers in Ireland, but so long as capitalists control the production process, retooling lives or dies on the whim of the market. *Power Systems and the Renewable Energy Transition* highlights how the constant tendency of capital to replace living labour with fixed capital and eject workers from production plays out in the renewable energy transition. There are not thousands of green jobs on every wind farm - there are a handful. The technical composition of renewable energy production is not suited to mass employment.

These barriers to the dream of a just transition are part of the constraints baked into the concept. First, the control of political power by the capitalist state, and second, the organisation of production through capitalist social relations. Parts of the ruling class understand well that 'for some things to remain the same, everything must change.' There are elements of the ruling class, particularly those with connections to the institutions of global governance, that want to integrate workers into a capitalist transition by offering crumbs of justice. But this pro-transition fraction is not at all dominant. On a general level, capital is not co-opting the pressure for green transition. Fossil capital and its allies are stonewalling.

In practice, workers' experience of energy transition is being forced through as a failed market intervention by the state. In Port Talbot, a steel community is being decimated by the introduction of electric arc furnaces. In Luton, the electric vehicle mandate is one of the excuses bosses give for relocating production to Turkey. In Grangemouth, the closure of the oil refinery and loss of 500 jobs is blamed on the energy transition. Again and again, "action" on carbon emissions is being felt as job losses and deindustrialisation, a process that echoes the deliberate assaults of Thatcherism decades before. The danger is that this looming axe persuades workers in carbon-intensive industries that all climate action only ever amounts to a state-led attack on them and their communities. One response to this could then be to ally with fossil capital in defence of their current form of exploitation. After all, in capitalism, the only thing worse than being exploited is not being exploited at all.

Vauxhall workers protest against a threatened plant closure in Luton. December 2024.

When we say a just transition is not and will not happen, are we suggesting that we should embrace the death drive? Not at all. Only by recognising that "Just

Transition" is a utopian demand can we face up to what we really need to do. So long as capitalist states and international institutions hold political power, there will be no just transition. What "successful" decarbonisation there is will continue to take the form of anti-working class assaults experienced as deindustrialisation, casualisation, and immiseration. In the near term, we will be struggling amid the chaos of a market-led non-transition. Instead of building castles in the air, we need to build power on the shopfloor. Then, when our chance comes, we can transition more than just the energy system.

The communist future in our current class struggles

The only realistic transition on the table is a communist transition. There is no singular programme or instruction manual for such a transition. The process itself will be shaped by the struggles taking place before and during it. The process of communist revolution will, by necessity, reshape the social masses of the world, and, in turn, will be reshaped by them.[3]

We can, however, learn from the historical attempts at communist transition in the contact of contemporary class composition. This can provide perspectives of what has *not* worked, and what could be done to build the form of political organisation that can move our struggles in a revolutionary direction. The experiences of workers' today, such as those highlighted in this issue, are vital to such an analysis. Not only must they inform abstract theories of revolution, but they must also be used to test whether they can work in practice. The tactics currently employed in working-class struggles must inform our political strategies, if we wish to influence and intensify their development towards revolutionary ends. Any potential political organisation must speak to this conveyor belt between tactics and strategy, between class struggle and political organisation.

Thinking through revolutionary strategy today has to be an intentional project that uses antagonisms at work to openly challenge capitalist control of society, while also consciously expanding outwards. It must be one that actively understands the current chains of production and reproduction in society, aiming to reproduce its forms of struggle along them. It is one in which the social hierarchies that dominate our workplaces and wider society must be subject

---

3   These questions are discussed in much greater detail by Phil. A Neel and Nick Chavez in *Forest and Factory The Science and the Fiction of Communism*. https://endnotes.org.uk/posts/forest-and-factory

to an active project of elimination. In James's words, "every tube driver is a cleaner, every cleaner is a tube driver." This abolition of social hierarchies in key industries must happen along with a move away from production governed by surplus value extraction towards that of social need. New political structures need to be formed to coordinate between bodies of workers in free association. In placing these inquiries into different industries side by side, we thus also raise the imperative of finding a means to coordinate activity across these industries, which collectively constitute the infrastructure of our economy. The inclusion of international inquiries from Sweden, Turkey, Ireland, and Slovenia in this issue is not solely a means to discover applicable lessons for more local struggles, but also reflects that we must fight the exploitation and violence which weaves together our inescapably global systems of energy and infrastructure.

This also means confronting the ideologies which operate through workforces to uphold existing command structures. As the contribution by *Gruvkvinnor* demonstrates, organisational autonomy oriented around feminist and rank-and-file principles can expose how patriarchy is not only embedded in the organisation of work (and the makeup of particular workforces), but also constitutes an ideological domain where the interests of male workers and bosses converge. From this perspective, workplace struggles for equality are not secondary to workers' efforts to control production. Instead, they are essential for dismantling the ideologies that reinforce capitalist control over the production process on a daily basis.

Through these processes, the consent which stems from disciplinary coercion and ideological segmentation, and which underpins the reproduction of capitalism, can be challenged at a broader societal level. Only on this basis is a communist transformation of production and society possible. Our day-to-day workplace organising and interventions in larger workers' struggles need to be geared towards this wider ambition.

Today, the stakes of worker control over the organisation and function of production have planetary ramifications. But the barriers to this collective responsibility seem impossibly high, and are mounting even higher. After years of relentlessly injecting competition, flexibility, and austerity, into every crevice of the social fabric, neoliberalism has generalised dysfunction and disintegration across many areas of infrastructural and reproductive work. The consequences for worker control are often clear to see. In the NHS, for example, decades of competing and contradictory management and policy agendas have produced a behemoth. This way of running a national health service is incompatible with even the most top-down technocratic oversight, not to mention democratic control.

The capitalist organisation of work and production is not simply a less equitable way of doing things. It is also a way of doing things that damages our capacity to recover the conditions of social production and reproduction for communist horizons. Along with professions dealing directly with the maintenance of human life (care, health, domestic work, and so on), those devoted to the maintenance of natural life most starkly reveal the political implications of how work is organised (or disorganised). In *Worker Based Solution to the Water Crisis* and *Something in the Water,* we see how capital fragments land and labour. This division hinders our ability to address the systematic issues of aquatic ecologies. It is also accelerating damage that cannot be undone. However, we should not understand this as a cause for nihilistic retreat. Instead, this is the stake of viewing struggle over the organisation and function of work as an ever-present imperative in workplace politics, even while acknowledging its limits as an ultimate end.

Political organisation

The question of how we get from where we are now to where we want to be is central. This is a question of political organisation. In their contribution, the comrades in CEDRA offer important lessons about how to develop from the failures of previous organisational forms. Ana, Živa and Marja describe the frustration and limitations of being in parties that focused on winning elections over building a working class base. And so, coming out of this experience, they state that:

> The initial idea behind CEDRA was thus: rather than forming a political party with a socialist program and then bringing this program to the working class in the form of the party, we should first offer help with workers' organising in various sectors and form organic connections.

This process of approaching the working class not as 'saviours sent from providence', but as comrades in struggle gave them the first steps back towards organisation.[4] The working class is not an identity to be represented in our organisations, but the fundamental functionary in the production and reproduction of society. Building working class bases is a strategic necessity.

---

4   Karl Marx (1880) *A Workers' Inquiry*, https://www.marxists.org/archive/marx/works/1880/04/20.htm

However, this is not to ignore the importance of identity in building working class organisation across class segmentations. As the autonomist feminist organising from *Gruvkvinnor* and CEDRA show, the objective conditions of production can offer a site to contest the subjective conditions of both production and reproduction, which develops a more general contestation to capitalist domination.

Political organisation is a process of composition and decomposition. It cannot be solved with a simple decision. There is no switch to turn "The Party" on or off. As the CEDRA comrades argue: 'political unity of the working class is not achieved automatically, and its form is never given once and for all.' The process of inquiry is essential here. This is an approach that opens up working class experience and develops the first steps of organisation. As class composition shifts and changes, an inquiry also needs to be iterative.

CEDRA use feminist co-research to develop new organisation in the retail sector in Slovenia, particularly in supermarkets. As we learned from a supermarket worker in the UK who contributed to issue 18 *Seeds Of Struggle*[5], this work is gruelling, technologically intensified, and often involves more work for less pay. Supermarket work is very different from the labour of other contributors in this issue. It is important to include the results of CEDRA's inquiry in this issue to highlight their approach of using inquiry to build political organisation within and beyond the immediate issues of production.

CEDRA has also developed a unique strategic analysis regarding the role of struggles over social reproduction in class political struggle more broadly. As the cost of living for the working class is tied directly to the industrial leverage of supermarket workers, building worker power at the meeting points of essential needs reveals the inherent contradictions of capitalist control over critical sites of social reproduction. In this way, workers' lives across the class are implicated in a particular set of workplace struggles, opening to a politicisation of profit-making and exploitation at the point of production and consumption. This strategic insight holds just as much relevance for struggles within the private utilities sectors.

---

5   An anonymous Supermarket Worker (2023) 'Work Well for Less', *Notes from Below*, https:// notesfrombelow.org/article/work-well-less-supermarket-inquiry

This is an essential reminder of the potential of workplace organising to lead to new possibilities. As Mike Davis puts it: 'organising campaigns and strikes have a politico-moral momentum that necessarily exceeds the economic demands that were their first cause'[6]. Engels described workers' struggles as "schools of war." He argued that we learn necessary lessons for a more complex political class war through the skirmishes of worker struggle.

Through reading the contributions from comrades organising in infrastructure in this issue, we can see how many challenges there are to building new and effective political organisations. As NfB editor Sai Englert laid out in issue 19, this should remind us of the pitfalls of 'understanding the vanguard not as a social relation, which is to say as a layer of militants that are more prepared than the average worker to fight back and get organised, but as an expression of specific political positions.'[7]

The narrative of "crumbling infrastructure" in Britain is a political fact, not an inevitability. It is in the absence of a counter-political expression that this crumbling occurs. The answer here is not slogans or programmes, but the organisation of workers who are ready to fight back. Inquiry is a way to find and, more importantly, organise with that militant layer.

Building our own infrastructure

As workers, we can see the process of infrastructural decline up close. We can see who makes the decisions that create it, how exploitation accelerates it, and the effects on our class. We are all involved in struggles to defend ourselves and fight for something better in the middle of this larger process. Sometimes, we fight in the open with unions and banners. Other times, we might fight below ground with hidden means. Either way, we are fighting just the same. But these struggles do not have a simple answer to that process of decline. Workers' control that doesn't challenge the mode of production gets reorientated by the demands of the market and competition. Resistance and refusal that proposes no alternative gets bogged down in endless fights with no larger horizon. Social democratic visions of just transition get caught up in the utopian "realism" of progressive transformation without the need for revolution. Every halfway house has its own structural flaws.

---

6   Mike Davis (2018) *Old Gods, New Enigmas: Marx's Lost Theory*, London: Verso.

7   Sai Englert (2023) 'Notes on Organisation - Revisited', Notes from Below, https://notesfrombelow.org/article/notes-organisation-revisited

So, we need to avoid stopping halfway. Communist transition is the only way out of this decline. This transition cannot be planned in advance. The early bourgeoisie were not working to a well-defined plan when they ground down feudalism over centuries. We are not working to a plan either. Real struggles over concrete questions will determine the course of the transition. These struggles will take place on the basis of the world that exists right now. Communist society will be built, as Marx and Engels put it, 'from the premises now in existence.'[8] That is to say, we will have to deal with the chaos that capitalism leaves behind. This chaos will create extreme challenges that threaten to pull us back into that mode of production, even as it begins to be overcome. The role of working class political organisation will not only be to start the transition to communism, but to defend it against counterrevolution.

Creating a political organisation is far from a simple or obvious process. An isolated minority should not just declare the new organisation or party. It has to be produced through struggle. Bit by bit, inquiry helps us to see what that process might look like. The groups of workers who are concentrated at key infrastructural points and engaged in practical militancy are likely to play a vital role in the process of organisation. Our hope is that this issue takes us one step closer to understanding how that recomposition can happen.

---

8   Karl Marx (1845) *German Ideology*, https://www.marxists.org/archive/marx/works/1845/german-ideology/ch01a.htm#p48

Under London

James

James is a train driver on the London Underground. He has worked there for over ten years, and is also a local representative for the RMT in his workplace.

I'm a train operator on the London Underground (LU) and a member of the RMT (National Union of Rail, Maritime and Transport Workers). I've worked here for over ten years. London Underground (LU) is a wholly owned subsidiary of Transport for London (TFL), which manages the day to day operation of the Underground. Industrially we are organised into one collective bargaining unit, so all 14,000 (approximately) directly employed workers bargain together and strike together over things like pay and terms and conditions. 10,000 of these workers are RMT members. Another 1800 are ASLEF members, a drivers only craft union. TSSA have a few hundred station staff, and UNITE organise in engineering with around 1000 members. I will look at what a day at work for a train operator is like, followed by a brief overview of recent disputes we have had in our workplace, then go on to examine how some of the work of producing a public transport system is organised and how it could look different under workers control.

The working day for an LU driver can start at any time between 04.30am and 11:55pm. We work a five day week, with two days off every week, with your total weekly working time not exceeding 36 hours. Each driver is only trained to work on their specific line, due to differences in the rolling stock on each line and different types of signal operation. Each line has train depots where drivers book on for work. For baby lines like the Bakerloo they have only two at Elephant & Castle and Queens Park, whereas bigger lines like the Northern have four. You book on with a train manager at your shift start time, you then have an agreed time until you pick up your train, which for us is 17 minutes. These times have been negotiated with management over the years and include agreed walking times from your booking on point to the location of the train. You may have heard these kind of agreements referred to as "Spanish practices" during recent train company strikes. But when your entire working day is structured by a timetable as it is for a train operator, you need the protection of agreed travel time, as every delayed train is looked into by a duty reliability manager to apportion blame for the delay. The normal working day is 8 hours, split into two halves from around 3 hours 30 mins to 4 hours 15 mins, with a meal break of 30 mins to 1 hour in between. We have a maximum agreed driving time of 4 hours and 15 mins without a break, and this along with other driving parameters are all written down in our agreements. These are learned verbatim by drivers over the years to protect yourself from line controllers who will always try to get more work out of you. The line controller is responsible for the overall management of the train service day to day, they sit in a central control room and communicate with drivers and other staff via radio. When the service is running as planned they have a relatively easy time, but, as anyone who uses the tube knows, we have plenty of unplanned events, it's then the line controllers job to get the service back to good, after signal failures etc. This is the main point of conflict for drivers when at work. The line controller wants certain trains in certain positions in order to get the service back to good, and you want to finish work on time and in the location you are supposed to. These two desires don't always match up. This is where we use our agreed driving parameters to assert ourselves over instructions from management. Or as the Tories would cry, "Spanish practices"!

The RMT nationally is divided up into geographical regions for organising. The London Transport Region (LTR), contains most workers organised under the TFL umbrella, with notable exceptions for London Overground and the Elizabeth Line. There are seventeen branches inside the LTR. Station and train staff share branches generally organised around a line (for example, Central Line West and Central line East), as well as grade specific branches for Fleet (train maintenance) and Engineering (track and signal maintenance). The branch is the democratic lynch pin of the union. Ideally you would have mass participation in branches. Even though we work in a heavily unionised workplace with union membership being over 90% for many grades, branch participation is low. Unfortunately most colleagues approach the union through the service model: I pay the union a fee, they provide me with services, if the union tells me to go on strike, I will. Local reps then become viewed as the representative of the union in the workplace. We are regularly asked questions along the lines of "what is the union position on this?", or "what is the union going to do about this?", rather than thinking of the union as a collective project where we come together to decide what we want, what we need and what we are willing to fight for.

This service model is one which British trade unions have slipped into over the decades since the historic defeat of the miners in the 1980s and with the continuous passing of anti union legislation, which has all been acquiesced to by the trade union movement without any real fight. The lack of democratic participation in branches suits the interests of union bureaucrats looking to occupy positions in the union without being challenged or even disposed of. This attitude can even lead to new people attending branch meetings as being viewed with suspicion. Having said all this, it still remains a relatively simple process to get strike action put on inside the RMT: a resolution calling for strike action needs to be put through a branch meeting which then goes to the union's National Executive Committee (NEC) for ratification, which has a culture of not refusing requests for strike ballots.

The past four years since the pandemic have seen the train operating companies and the government launch a number of coordinated attacks against workers, using the drop off in fares during COVID as a justification to push for cuts to terms and conditions. The peak of these disputes was a combined London Underground and national rail strike on 21st June 2022, where 40,000 national rail staff were joined by 10,000 London underground workers. This was the first time since the privatisation of the railways in the 1990s where there has been a combined shutdown of London tube services and national rail trains. Unfortunately this was the only day where this national action was used. After this, the various disputes were hived off to fight separately, with Network Rail settling their dispute in March 2023. RMT station and train staff were left to fight on alone with seemingly random one day strikes organised now and again, none of which were coordinated with ASLEF drivers who were also calling a succession of one day strikes. These two pay disputes were strung out until the election of a Labour government, where they were settled for an ever so slightly better offer, that proved to be more acceptable to union bureaucracy as it was wrapped in a red ribbon.

On the London Underground, rank and file reps looked at the ineffectiveness of one day strikes being taken by both ASLEF and RMT on national rail, and came up with a new format of strikes for the underground. This new format looked to shut the tube for a week, using different grades going out on different days through the week, so each grade would only lose two days of pay, but the strike would affect seven days of tube service - effectively seven days of strike action for the price of two. This is where having an industrially organised union fighting in the same collective bargaining unit gives workers an organisational advantage over craft unions fighting in sectional disputes (NHS workers, take note please). This seven day strike has now been named three times - in August 2023, January 2024 and November 2024 - and all 3 times it has been called off at the very last minute. In only one of these instances, January 2024, was the strike called off for what was a significantly improved pay offer: two days into the strike the Mayor offered an extra £30 million for pay to call the rest of the strike off.

This year's 2024 pay negotiations are still ongoing in November, and the pay rise was due in the May 2024 pay packet. This delay always advantages the company, as back pay owed increases as the negotiations continue. The negotiations this year centred around TFLs attempt to break up the LU collective bargaining unit into smaller groups of "job families" - a classic piece of neo-liberal management guru doublespeak. These conditions were eventually dropped from the pay offer, which left an actual pay offer which averaged out at 4.6%, however this was weighted to be slightly more for lower paid grades, leaving higher paid grades below RPI inflation for Feb 2024. At a well attended reps meeting on October 30th, this offer was deemed not good enough and it was agreed that the strike, which was starting on 1st November, should remain on. In spite of this outcome from the all reps meeting, the seven day strike was pulled by the RMT NEC on the morning of 1st November. At the time of writing this decision still seems to be a bit of mystery. The decision to pull the strikes was accompanied with a communication from Mick Lynch that a "significantly improved offer" had been made, the actual details of which are yet to materialise. This sort of "union" intervention into disputes to call off strikes last minute without any consultation is exactly the kind of action which leads people into the service model relationship with their union: one where the union makes the decisions, and we, the workers, follow.

The democracy of a union and the levels of worker participation are a work in progress, and always have room for improvement - but compared to the authoritarian dictatorship that is the capitalist workplace, they are revolutionary. The model in union branch structures, reps elected to time limited roles, and voting on resolutions, can give a glimpse of how a revolutionary workplace could be managed. The culture is in place where it could be transferred from a branch to a workplace council, where debate around how to democratically manage work and mass participation should hopefully be much easier, given the free time available to workers freed from capitalist work time directives. There already exists some workers self-management in train depots, as currently we have what are called "syndicates". This is where the allocation of driving duties is given over to another train operator who is then given time away from train driving every week to organise the duties. The rules of this are set out in a LU document called syndicate guidelines. Where I work there are 150 drivers, with a 95 week long roster. You can swap any duty with any other driver weekly, by filling out a mutual changeover of duty form. However, management simply would not have the time to process all these duty swaps. So the company agreed to leave this changeover of duties in the hands of the train operator assigned to the syndicate, whom we have called the mafia man/woman - mafia and syndicate being interchangeable, of course. Their job is to keep a list of what each driver wants (start times, rest days etc.) and then assign the duties every week in order to give everybody what they have asked for. The mafia person will need to be someone who is agreeable to most in the depot, and they will need to keep most of the depot happy in order to maintain high participation in their mafia. There have been situations where competing mafias have been set up in the same depot when drivers haven't been happy. A well-run mafia means that instead of working the roster - where start times vary from 4:30am, 5pm or night shifts starting at 11pm - drivers can choose a relatively consistent start time, leading to a much healthier sleep pattern and reducing fatigue, stress and sickness. Although this is a little glimmer of workers' self-management, I don't think colleagues imagine our syndicate as an example of how a post-revolutionary workplace could be managed. This is probably due to a distinct lack of imagining a new world on all our parts.

There are roughly 27,000 people directly employed under the TFL umbrella, according to their workplace monitoring report of 2016. 15,327 of these are employed in operational roles, such as drivers, station staff, and engineers. 11,108 are employed in support roles "providing administrative, specialist and policy guidance". Are these 11,000 bullshit jobs? As somebody who works on the operational side, I couldn't begin to imagine what these 11,000 people actually do. A quick example of some of the job titles in TFL doesn't really help us get an understanding of their role in running trains and buses. Director of People Operations, Employee Relations and Rewards, Head of TFL Change, Chief People Officer, Director of Diversity and Inclusion, Head of Change Portfolio Office, Head of Employee Comms and Engagement. In an attempt to give some credit to these departments, I did look up TFL change on our intranet to try to figure out what they do. It appears their role is to convince the workforce that proposed changes are actually good for us. "Change" in this context is nearly always, for operational staff, an increase in your workload, increase in time at work, worsening of rosters etc. The change management guidance produced by the Change Department includes a diagram called *"The change curve - understanding the emotional journey of change"*, and other such pearls of wisdom. This diagram includes a line which says:

"A structured business change approach aims to smooth the curve to minimise the time spent in the dip of the curve and also to ensure that people reach enthusiasm and commitment faster."

Pretty much all the restructuring changes that have come out of the change department in the past four years have been knocked back with strike action, so I guess this means we are stuck permanently in the dip of the emotional curve, disillusionment. I am of the belief that we could run a public transport service without "a structured business approach to managing the emotional journey of change". Work under capitalism is authoritarian and hierarchical, and as such always leads to conflict. The attempt to manage this conflict leads then to this ever expanding field of human resources that asks: how do we manage these humans to get them to do things that are simultaneously boring and exhausting? A post-revolutionary workplace would surely have to free us from the meaningless guff of human resources, both for those who work under it and in it, because the people writing the "change management" guidance must hate it even more than the people reading it.

There are probably roles in amongst these 11,000 support workers that would still need to be done in a post-capitalist workplace - procurement of materials and parts being one - but undoubtedly the disciplined focus management administration side could be done away with. If this figure of 40% of workers inside TFL "supporting" the operational side are mirrored across other industries, then that is a vast number of workers who could be retrained and help reduce time spent at work for all.

These directly employed LU staff are then backed up by an army of outsourced more precariously employed workforce of 3000 cleaners who are outsourced to ABM (American Building Maintenance), security staff to Mitie, canteen staff to Serco, maintenance staff to Close Brothers, and track staff to Cleshars. The list of outsourced companies employed under LU is almost endless and is further complicated when many of the outsourced companies further outsource work again, especially for work deemed unprofitable for them. The RMT organises across all these employers, and will have members everywhere, but union density is much lower amongst the outsourced staff, and as a result so is organisation. There have been various attempts made over my ten years working here to organise these workers, which have primarily focused on the cleaning grade. These have normally been led by the organising department in the RMT with help from directly employed activists and a few cleaner activists as well. These efforts have run up against the usual obstacles to organising a diverse precariously employed workforce. The workplace itself spans the entire city, with cleaners based at every station in London and every train depot. Visiting different workplaces as activists to recruit becomes laborious, you could spend a day traveling the city to talk to only ten cleaners. Where we have directly employed activists and reps who work alongside cleaners and see it as their role to organise cleaners as well is where we see the best results. We have recently won a recognition agreement with ABM, which for the first time means we can elect cleaner reps which will be recognised by their employer, meaning facility time and a machinery of negotiation. There is still a long way to go, but having a cadre of cleaner reps representing other cleaners will hopefully help break the mindset of many outsourced staff that the union is only for directly employed staff.

For anybody who works in the public sector and has encountered trying to navigate the labyrinthine complexity of networks of outsourced employers, the idea that this system is more efficient or productive is laughable. How many outsourced London Underground workers does it take to change a light bulb? Maybe four, and a large payment from the public purse to the private sector. If I find a problem in my workplace, let's say a blocked toilet, I report it to my line manager who then raises it as a job at the centralised TFL fault reporting centre. They then create a job number and file and will then send it to one of the outsourced maintenance contractors, probably Close Brothers. They may send one of their directly employed staff to fix it, or they may outsource the job again to a smaller contractor. Close Brothers are paid the same flat fee every month to respond to these small scale jobs, so the more work they do in a month the less profit they make. Therefore the profit margins inside such contracts involve avoiding work, doing it late, doing it badly and then relying on poor record keeping or reporting in TFL to get away with this. Even something as simple as getting the toilets cleaned has to follow a similar process, with the cleaning contractor ABM also incentivised to employ the least amount of staff possible in order to maximise profit. Obviously the skill set exists in the 28,000 staff TFL directly employs to change light bulbs and clean toilets - these outsourcing facility companies offer no special expertise. These sorts of contracts don't even make sense under capitalism, with each outsourced company having to reproduce the management, payroll, HR departments multiple times over. Each outsourced contract is simply a way for public sector dosh to be turned into profit, rather than a job with sick pay, pension and security of position.

A post-revolutionary train depot would hopefully be able to deal with a dirty or blocked toilet far more efficiently than this, with no such artificial division of labour necessary between cleaners or drivers. Workers' self-management would mean dealing with such problems ourselves as they arise, every driver a cleaner, every cleaner a driver, with no need to sign a multi-million pound contract with a multinational facilities management provider to get our toilets cleaned.

Mine women: how we organised an independent movement of female mine workers in Sweden

Gruvkvinnor

We are a group of mine working women who started an independent women's organisation called Gruvkvinnor [Mine women] in the northern part of Sweden a few years ago. Most of us work, or have been working in Kiruna for a state owned company called LKAB. They operate the biggest underground iron ore mine in the world and the company supplies the whole of Europe with minerals.

Kiruna is located in a region with a big mining industry called Malmfälten. LKAB is the largest iron ore company in the region and operates three mines within an area of 120 kilometers. The Kiruna mine employs 1500 workers and about 20 percent of them are women. There are also a large number of subcontractors who carry out work on behalf of LKAB. Women also work in these companies, but they are much fewer in number.

The group was founded in October 2018 but the work did not start then. Blue collar-working women had experienced unequal working conditions and sexual harassment for a long time. For example, our working clothes and shoes were not available in small sizes. The toilets were not equipped with running water so it was hard to change menstrual protection in a hygienic way. Pregnant women and parents were also discriminated against. The work tasks were adapted to men and it was a struggle every day to be respected by the male workers and management.

We felt that there was no one representing us on these issues - neither from the trade union nor from the company. We had no trust for the trade union organisation, as it also consisted mainly of men and had not previously shown any interest in these types of issues.

After many discussions with a lot of women at different workplaces we decided that something needed to be done. We were convinced that these issues were best addressed by women who experience the problems themselves, but we also believed in an organisation consisting only of blue collar working women. We wanted to ensure that no manager could attend the meetings and hear the women stories, creating a culture of insecurity and silence. We wanted to create a safe place where they would be able to raise their voice. We wanted free discussions and mutual understanding. We welcomed all women in production, regardless of company, so even if you worked for the parent company LKAB, cleaned the premises or were a mechanic for a subcontractor, you were welcome. This is not something the traditional trade unions do in Sweden, as their organising is restricted to different collective agreements that divide the employees at the workplaces.

Gruvkvinnor's goal was to unite all these women to improve working conditions for all, and especially in matters related to the female body. But we did not consider ourselves opponents to the male part of the workforce, and believed the issues we pushed would also benefit them. For example, all the changing rooms at LKAB were renovated. Later we won a contractual change where men were given the opportunity to accompany their partners to the midwife during paid working hours.

Swedish Trade Unionism

It is important to understand how the Swedish trade union movement functions to understand why we decided to be independent from them. The Swedish trade union is very bureaucratised and strictly governed by by-laws and regulations. The trade unions in Sweden are an integral part of the Swedish labour market. The membership rate is around 70 percent, which is a high figure compared to the rest of the world. Most companies have signed a collective agreement where the unions have negotiated specific conditions for workers in the same industry regardless of the factory they work in. These agreements regulate, for example, working hours, wages and vacations. In any large industrial company, there are always several formally elected people working full-time on trade union issues only. But elections are tightly controlled from above and these people become very close to the company management. Many sit on the company boards.

One of the problems with this is that the unions are not very present in workplaces as they spend more time at the negotiating table with managers than with the union members. Many collective workers have lost trust in these formal representatives.

So why did we not want to be a part of the trade union apparatus with such a high membership? If we had become a part of the trade union apparatus, our hard work would have gone to waste immediately. Because of the strict bureaucracy we would not have been able to organise other women besides miners, and we would not have been able to organise women only. All of this is strictly regulated and we did not want to be limited in our work. Our main focus was the blue-collar women and their rights. To be a part of the trade union apparatus would not change any of their working conditions for the better.

First Initiatives and Building the Organisation

Our first meeting invitation was sent out as a text message that was passed on between different women. The first meeting was located in a basement room that we had borrowed. The goal for the meeting was to gather as many working women as possible. We wanted to meet women from different parts of the mining industry to see if there were others who felt discriminated against and overlooked. Women of different ages, from different companies and from different parts of production attended the meeting. We already felt there was a great need for us to pursue these issues and many were interested and committed to work further.

From that week on, a small but tight group worked very closely. We met several times a week to get the work going. Our hard work led to a #metoo leaflet with testimonies from female miners in Malmfälten. The leaflet was spread throughout LKAB's mining area and we involved many to distribute them. The work site encompasses several thousand employees, both in the parent company and subcontractors. The aim was to reach out to male workers and show them a few examples of the sexual abuse, harassment and discrimination that women in the mine industry experienced. To distribute over a thousand leaflets in an industrial area, 3 kilometers in diameter, with operations both above and below ground, is quite difficult. This was only possible because we had a large number of people helping us with everything from layout, printing, premises and distribution. This was a collective effort in which both women and men from the mining community helped to reach as many people as possible.

That was the start of an organisation that became much bigger than we had hoped for. We had found a gap that needed to be filled.

We continued our work and created working groups that focused on various women-related issues. These working groups were put together by people who felt dedicated to a certain question. The #metoo-leaflet is an example of one of our first working groups. Gruvkvinnor had decided at a meeting, where all blue collar working women from the mining industry were invited, that a leaflet should be put together. The women who felt motivated and engaged to do it became a working group with the goal of creating and distributing the leaflet. The people inside the group worked closely together with meetings almost every week. The work included collecting testimonies from female workers, writing them down on paper, putting it all together, laying out the leaflet, printing it and finding people to distribute them. Afterwards the group summarised the work at a feedback meeting to evaluate the action and decide how to continue.

Except for the #metoo-testimonies, the most prioritised issues were the matters of parental leave, pregnancy and breastfeeding. Working groups were also created around these subjects. In this way of working we attracted women who were interested in working on one, or a few specific questions, but maybe not participate in every single one. We had several working groups running parallel to each other. In this way we got more efficient and it was easier to make people participate when they got to choose what kind of issue to get involved in.

We created a private Facebook-group so we could gather all the working women on one specific platform. We made our invitation through the Facebook-page and a lot of important information was shared through that channel. It became a communication forum where everyone could speak, and later on it also became an archive with our protocols and statutes.

We studied health and safety legislation so we would have more knowledge and facts than our counterparts. We took the initiative to invite the formal trade union representatives from all over the region to discuss these problems with the aim of setting a common goal for gender equality work. This was a way of pressuring the unions, and in turn the companies, to work for the demands we made. No one had more knowledge than we did, nor did anyone have better arguments, which meant that we walked out victorious from these types of meetings.

We also introduced our own Women's Representatives, who were to be independently elected by the work mates, to safeguard the workplaces and serve as a link between the group and the collective. These representatives were only elected by women, and all the issues that were put in the hands of these representatives were handled by women only. This was not appreciated by the company and union. The company claimed that we did not have this right, and the union felt that we were trespassing into their territory. This was not something that could have existed within the framework of the trade union, as it does not allow separate organisation.

Independent organisation gave us a freedom that we would not have had anywhere else. We have achieved a lot of important changes in the mining industry during these years. For example, we forced LKAB to repay women who had been discriminated against during their pregnancies a total amount of over 100,000 euro. We became the ones who represented the majority of our members in the workplace, we started a podcast and we negotiated on specific issues with LKAB. We also saw a change in the attitude towards women. A lot of discrimination in workplaces ended.

Much of the work we did was located in the womens' changing room, a place where both workers for the subcontractors and LKAB change clothes every day. We centered a lot of our work and communication in that area because barely any managers changed in our dressing rooms, and it was a place where almost all blue collar women passed through every day. So this was a strategically useful place to spread information and have confidential conversations. The second thing is that we prevented ourselves from being a service unit, meaning that almost every woman working on the site was close to our every day work. They heard conversations about issues we were pushing for, which made it much easier to get involved. We put up posters inside the changing rooms and we distributed a lot of information from there. It was a safe space for us and we reached the majority of workers from just one premise.

Above we mention all of our achievements, but we have not won all battles and every demand we pushed for has required a large amount of work. One disadvantage of being independent from the union apparatus was that we had no financial means other than the money that came from our own pockets. The companies and the trade unions have a lot more power when it comes to money. This was not all negative though, as the women who chose to get involved in the group felt a great responsibility for the issues and the work we did. As we had no financial contributors to consider, we were completely free to shape our own policy. The workers never had to doubt whom we represented and where we had our loyalty.

But the financial advantage of our opponents - which in this case were LKAB, the subcontractors and also the trade unions - became a quite significant problem. All of them put in a lot of money to block our progress in various ways. For example, LKAB chose to pay a union representative whose sole task was to work on gender equality issues. There were no elections for this position, the person was appointed entirely by the company and the union, which shows that they were probably very concerned about our progress. This was a way for them to maneuver us out of their playing field. As soon as they had weakened us enough, this full-time appointment was done away with.

Gruvkvinnor was growing and we knew our big support had made us powerful. We had a lot of women representatives and we pushed through with more demands. It was an intense period when our work started to pay off and we grew bigger pretty quickly. Our spokesperson got to participate in Sweden's largest radio show with an audience of millions of listeners and we had ongoing negotiations with LKAB. The latter took a lot of energy from us. Negotiations are slow moving and easily gets you distracted from strategic considerations. It wasted energy and was not so successful.

Reflections

After these months, the small but somewhat more experienced core of the group started to weaken. We did not have the energy to organise and educate new members, so no one could relieve or replace us either. This is something we should have done differently. We should have focused more on the group, keeping up the good spirit and energy among the newcomers. It is hard to know what is best to do when no one has done it before you. Someone has to be first. And when it comes to gender equality work at LKAB and in the mining industry in Malmfälten, we can proudly say that we took the lead. We broke new ground for the position of women in a male-dominated world. But we could also have done it better.

Gruvkvinnor still exists, but we have worked really hard to keep up the activity ever since the pandemic. Almost all of our key players were exhausted at that time and it was hard to keep up the motivation during isolation. In the beginning we tried online meetings. We even tried meeting outside, in -15 degrees celsius sitting around a campfire. But when the pandemic seemed neverending it got really hard. The whole society was on hold. Our work too.
WNow we are trying to restart the group, because we know it is necessary for us to be out at workplaces.

We have evaluated our work and know that we made considerable change. We have educated women through struggles and it has been incredible to see a whole collective fighting for their rights. We have seen the sparks in women's eyes after successful battles and the camaraderies among us has created a safe place for so many. The community we created and the trust we got from so many workers were a big part of our achievements. We were not seasoned activists in the beginning but made it together. We have both victories and setbacks behind us, but the most important thing was that we supported each other along the way. We succeed because of our independent organisation.

Worker Based Solution to the Water Crisis.

An anonymous former environmental worker

This note from below is written by an environmental worker, who used to work for England's largest environmental regulator in communications.

The Water

Nowhere is the plundering and scorched-earth nature of late-stage capital so stark as in the case of water. The sewage pollution crisis is its visceral representation. Water companies operate a private monopoly that routinely spills raw, untreated sewage into inland and coastal waters, killing habitats, poisoning swimmers and the water supply (which they then must treat), whilst extracting huge profits through sweating assets and amounting debt, then shifting the economic burden onto the taxpayer. It is exactly as it seems – daylight robbery, class warfare and ecocide – but this is not even half the story.

While pollution from sewage treatment presents a significant threat to the health of water bodies and evokes a strong image in everyone's minds, diffused rural pollution is the largest contributor to their poor state[9]. Natural fertilisers, containing high amounts of chemical elements such as phosphorus and nitrogen, which act as nutrients for maximum crop yields, are frequently over-applied. This pollutes the soil, and the excess enters the water environment causing algal blooms and the starving of fish and invertebrates of oxygen. But this is not all. Most fertilisers are from slurry (animal shit), which often contain bacteria and pathogens, or they are off-site wastes such as sewage sludge (human shit) and are only partially treated for certain chemicals. This means things like medicines and illegal drugs etc. are frequently entered into the mix. Combined with pesticides or veterinary medicines, microplastics, industrial chemicals and those from personal care products, this creates what has been dubbed a 'chemical cocktail'[10], which is devastating non-human nature and having unknown effects on humans too.

---

9   https://committees.parliament.uk/publications/8460/documents/88412/default/

10   https://www.wcl.org.uk/chemical-cocktail-campaign.asp

Many potentially dangerous effects of these chemicals are not being identified, let alone screened and then treated.[11] Along with keeping delicate ecosystems in balance, this water is then consumed either in everyday domestic human use, or industrial processes. This includes in food production, cleaning and watering of plants, consumption by livestock, as an ingredient, or in manufacturing or energy production, to be used for cooling, heating or cleaning, and much more. But its management and health has entered a period of acute crisis, which has implications for us all. This is particularly concerning because, as water becomes increasingly scarce it also becomes harder to predict and control, which is no coincidence. We're taking too much. Too much is being lost and this contributes to global heating, which then returns in almost yearly record-breaking downpours – floods – or disappears for long periods of intense heat – drought – which have devastating effects on human health, livelihoods, infrastructure and everything else.

However, whether the source of pollution is agriculture or water companies, whether it is scarce because of leaks in the system, or over-abstraction[12], it is the result of de-regulation and non-regulation.

The Worker

From the perspective of the worker in the environmental regulator, it doesn't feel like there's a lack of regulation. It feels like you're doing something, or more often, doing too much. Plus, there's tens of thousands of you, if you count all the environmental regulator workers in Britain. Furthermore, the organisation that you work for tells you that things are going well. Not only are we doing a lot – as the daily comms or calls suggest – but we're innovating all the time. Especially if you deal in issuing permits, answering phones or dishing out notices to rogue waste sites. There are loads of regulations. Maybe too many.

The workforce is large and a peculiar mix, its consciousness as eclectic as its regulatory portfolio. People are motivated by different things. As well as being a scientific advisor to government, the organisation is an advisor to and regulator of industry, an enforcer against crime, an emergency responder and licenser of recreational activity. As such, the workforce is drawn from multiple classes. There are working class field workers, administrators, phone handlers,

---

11   https://publications.parliament.uk/pa/ld5803/ldselect/ldindreg/166/16602.htm

12   For a definition of and to understand abstraction: https://www.castlewater.co.uk/blog/what-is-water-abstraction

and to a lesser degree, enforcement or regulatory people, who swiftly enter a new class position by virtue of higher pay, professionalisation or technical specialisation, and almost have a 'protected' status in the organisation. From amongst the middle classes – which are by far the largest group– there are scientists, civil engineers, project managers, policy wonks, an army of public relations professionals, business managers, analysts, regulators and enforcers. From amongst these layers, most of the senior management is drawn. Graduates, who may hail from middle class backgrounds, can enter the organisation in the lower grades, but are able to move upwards quite quickly due to longstanding recruitment and retention issues. For the working class graduates, there's less mobility but often a scientific background can help you cut through. The organisation is very white, though that is gradually changing due to company schemes but this doesn't go far enough. What continues to prevail is a hegemonic ideology of environmentalism, which comes with a great deal of paternalistic but socially 'progressive' attitudes towards both the environment and communities. This is sometimes overt, or covert, and is in the subtext of our activity: people and places are to be managed, because we know what's best for them.

Technically, many of the roles work to different rhythms. Inspections, sampling and maintenance usually takes place in daylight core hours by ecologists, industry regulators and operational staff, who work out of depots or labs in the near hinterland of the rural provinces. In all cases, it is seasonal. Either due to the meteorological seasons, which are in great flux and changing due to the climate, or due to regulatory and legislative requirements e.g. X amount of inspections must be conducted according to X date. To greater or lesser degrees, these workers spend time out in the field in gangs, working alone, or with partner organisations. It can be very dangerous work and in recent years, environmental workers have died due to slips and falls, and routinely fall ill due to the accidental inhalation or ingestion of toxic chemicals.[13]

Permitting, business planning, analysis of data, policy work, comms or customer support is largely office or home-based, and carried out by an array of professionals. While much of this work will be carried out according to various deadlines – which are increasing in number and coming about more quickly due to demands on resources, the environment and political pressures – they

---

13   It must be said that the employer takes health and safety seriously, but this has obvious, known limits and is not consistent across the whole organisation. There is somewhat of a mental health crisis for office staff and some workers must go to great lengths to obscure their identity so that organised criminals in the waste sector cannot track them down.

have a 'circadian rhythm' about them. These staff tend to enjoy a greater deal of flexibility in their work e.g. adjusted, flexible or reduced hours. This is a concession resulting from employers needing to keep pay low, but feeling the pressure to reward and adapt worker demands into a policy.

However, emergency or incident response – much like a strike – is the great leveller. Workers from all social and technical backgrounds might hold an incident role – typically suited to their specialism – and can be deployed when an environmental event e.g. flooding, waste fires, pollution spills etc. trigger the incident structures to 'scale up' and respond. This could be anything from officers taking sampling, operations workers deploying temporary flood barriers or admin staff operating incident rooms to coordinate resources. Every incident is different, even in respect to flooding, but often always largely relies on a paid voluntary force, who receive internal training and take turns to stand by on rosters. There are permanent incident staff, but they aren't many and in recent years there has been talk of making the incident spine more 'permanent'. This is because, as the impacts of climate change become more severe, there are nearly constant incidents requiring a response. This keeps the organisation in a perpetually reactive and attritional state, to the detriment of more proactive, 'business-as-usual' activities.

In the past, incident response has been a point of leverage for the trade unions - withdrawing from rosters has been used effectively as an action short of strike. It has historically been based on a lot of 'good will', which has been eroded by poor pay and treatment over time. It is no surprise then that since the first strikes over pay in the organisation's history, the business has made incident response 'contractually mandatory' for new starters. This press ganging into incident duties is being both over and underutilised in 'area' and 'national'.

But there is an understated effect of incident work too, which is that much like the strike, there is no feeling like it. Working incidents, like standing on picket lines, has a galvanising effect, which captures, inherently contains and generates an array of quite powerful emotional and ideological drivers. Many colleagues often have an instinctive sense of duty towards the public and the environment – the organisation is full of fantastic people. Deploying resources to keep communities safe, evacuating homes and liaising with distressed communities can be a profound experience, contributing to a sense of purpose and identity.

The Water

Water outlines the shape and reveals the depths of dysfunction. It's true that cuts have had a serious operational impact on the organisation and that they have been 'weaponised' to undermine its independence. In the case of water, inspections of sites (agriculture or utility) and monitoring of water bodies dropped off a cliff after 2010 and did not return to normal until the water quality crisis had become a national scandal and forced a new financial settlement. During this period, enforcement action disappeared, but 'ring-fenced' funding for the organisation's role as a planner and emergency responder to flood risk was secured.

De and re-regulation further complicate the mess. At the point when Con-Dem policies of privatisation and 'growth' began to take full effect, the country left the European Union (EU). There was also a surge in climate awareness, driven in the British context by mainly middle-class environmentalists such as Extinction Rebellion. New statutory requirements including headline environmental targets – EU legacy legislation – were established in UK law due (in part) to public pressure. Meanwhile greater power was centralised in government and other regulations were cut, unleashing the private sector on services.

Then comes the pandemic, grinding projects to a halt and having unknown effects on the climate. This opened onto a period of inflation, which forced the costs of construction, living, and labour upwards. As we emerge out of our homes and into this 'new normal', greater time is spent appreciating nature, bringing people into contact with the devastating effects of pollution in England's rivers, and making them sick and angry. The crisis becomes a national scandal. The result of all this on the environmental regulator is new and increased responsibilities under immense pressure which are increasingly delivered by parasitic outsourced providers. Although adequately funded for some work that is significantly delayed (for reasons beyond its control), the regulator is overall unbalanced because budget cuts have come at the expense of other services. The workforce is poorer and stretched, and, as a result, leave in droves to the private sector, settle for an early retirement or strike, hampering delivery, and contributing to a vacancy churn.

All this time, the situation for the environment and infrastructure intensifies and becomes more apparent. The organisation is not able to meet its target of maintaining 98% of its high consequence flood defences at their required condition, falling short by approximately 5%, and exposing more than 200,000 properties to increased risk.[14] Not a single reservoir for capturing and storing water has been constructed or meaningfully progressed, which means the government will not have completed a single major reservoir between 1991 and 2029. Meanwhile, approximately 51 litres of water per person per day is lost to leaks, the majority of which occur in pipes owned by private water companies.[15] With population increases and consumer behaviour unchanged, demand for water will outstrip supply in the next 20 years.[16] Further still, transference of water from saturated areas to those almost permanently under 'stress' is near impossible.

To inspect and fix assets, construct new reservoirs, and replace Victorian pipes pissing out precious water with a view to transfer it requires a huge amount of coordination and capital. One might naively think that a small cartel of large uncompetitive companies, making pre-tax profits of approximately £1.7 billion a year[17], would be well situated to do this. Instead, they have lined their pockets, paying out approximately £78 billion in dividends to shareholders[18], of which the pension fund for the environmental regulator is one.[19] Such an arrangement, which is deeply unpopular with workers in the regulator, means that they are directly implicated in and incentivised by the exploitation of the very environment they have devoted their careers to protecting. Further still, this entangles them in the fortunes of the companies themselves, as divestment could lead to their collapse due to the sector's vulnerability to market fluctuations. This is a likely possibility, as in the case of Thames Water, which has racked up around £14.7bn of debt and is near bankruptcy.[20]

---

14   https://committees.parliament.uk/work/7973/flood-defences/news/199357/flood-resilience-eroded-by-poorly-maintained-defences-with-government-in-the-dark-on-progress/

15   https://publications.parliament.uk/pa/ld5803/ldselect/ldindreg/166/16602.html

16   https://www.theguardian.com/environment/2023/mar/17/global-fresh-water-demand-out-strip-supply-by-2030

17   https://www.theguardian.com/business/2024/mar/15/water-firms-profits-england-wales-almost-double-since-2019

18   https://leftfootforward.org/2024/04/16-water-monopolies-have-paid-out-a-total-of-78bn-in-dividends-as-thames-water-teeters-on-the-brink/

19   https://www.theguardian.com/business/2022/aug/10/environment-agency-pension-fund-criticised-for-owning-stakes-in-uk-water-firms

20   https://www.theguardian.com/business/2024/apr/16/thames-water-to-ask-debt-markets-for-survival-plan-funding

Around 20%, or 20p for every pound paid by customers, goes to servicing the industry's £60.3bn debt mountain.[21] As it grows, the need to increase the rate of exploitation in labour, raw material, rents (bills) and sunk capital in assets does too. Although natural attrition due to most water workers nearing retirement age alongside a national skills shortage appears to have somewhat done the job for them, there is a deep contradiction between what the sector needs and what it can provide.

The Land

It is impossible to talk about water, without talking about land. Much of this is common-sense: water enters rivers or seas via the land, and its topology or saturation rate influences the quantity or velocity entering the body, and, as such, its shape, volume and flow. Land brings with it many pollutants; fuel from roads, sewage from combined overspills, chemicals sprayed on fields or nutrients from overloaded soil. This water is captured for storage or abstracted and drank by the consumer, or used by industry in processes for agriculture, construction or energy production. Any ecologist or hydrologist will tell you that there's good reason to study land in its own right, but none would deny water and land's inter-relatedness: for flood risk, for good soil health, for supply, biodiversity, lower water treatment costs, or health benefits etc.

But then one might sensibly ask: if the two are inextricably linked, then why are they often treated as being separate and distinct? The answer is: private property. It will be no surprise to any reader of *Notes from Below* that the practical, scientific, or common-sense relationship between water and land has little bearing on regulatory outcomes. A greater quantity, better supplied, or higher quality of water is contingent on who owns and controls it and why.

According to research by Guy Shrubsole – author of *Who Owns England* – just 1% of the population own half of the land in England, with the aristocracy or landed gentry still owning around a third. A good deal of this is agricultural land as approximately 67% of land is worked in England.[22] This could be for arable crops (such as vegetables, fruits or cereals), for livestock (sheep, cattle, chickens

---

21   https://www.theguardian.com/environment/ng-interactive/2023/dec/18/how-much-of-your-water-bill-is-swallowed-up-by-company-debt-interactive

22   Guy Shrubsole (2019) *Who Owns England?: How We Lost Our Green and Pleasant Land, and How to Take It Back*. London; William Collins

or pigs etc.), or for growing non-edible crops (flowers and plants).
Although according to some research approximately 14,500 hectares of
productive land (less than 1%) has been 'lost' to development since 2010[23],
and there is an incentive for some smaller farmers and landowners, usually on
the edges of towns or cities, to sell up for developers. There is, however, even
greater incentives for them to hold on to the land. For the price of land – as sure
as dawn breaking and night falling – appreciates. And this ensures, for the largest
landowners, the maintenance of power and generational wealth.

The number of small farms (under 100 hectares) has decreased by half in
the last 60 years and the number of small holdings has also decreased, from
approximately 160,000 in 1950 to less than 30,000 in 2020.[24] In the UK,
18% of farms are now 'large farms' and they control over 73.6% of farmland.[25]
Similarly in other areas of agriculture, these figures represent a clear trend
of monopolisation by larger family-run enterprises or corporate-entities.
Many farmers face tight margins and many of them are essentially unprofitable
(the 'average farm' makes 13 times more from subsidies than they do from
agriculture)[26], but there's a good deal of money swilling about in the agri-food
sector, £146.7 billion, in fact.[27] And as a sector which employs around 470,000
people[28], it would be wrong to focus on the tiny minority – the landowners – too
much, but the reality is that if you own the land, you own the water.

Private property rights grant landowners a huge amount of freedom on how they
use the land, especially that land which is not protected or does not have special
status. And while there is no absolute right to develop land, it's not stopping
many rural or semi-rural developments being built on flood plains, exposing
these homeowners to risk of flooding, but also contributing to higher flood
risk for others downstream or adjacent to them because it changes the surface
topology of the land, with less water being absorbed or stored and more being
directed to sewers, which can get overloaded more quickly. In turn, this forces

23   https://www.cpre.org.uk/wp-content/uploads/2022/07/Building-on-our-food-security.pdf

24   https://pipersfarm.com/blogs/journal/the-slow-disappearance-of-small-british-family-farms

25   https://www.gov.uk/government/statistics/agricultural-facts-england-regional-profiles/agricultural-facts-summary

26   https://fullfact.org/economy/farming-subsidies-uk/

27   https://www.gov.uk/government/statistics/agriculture-in-the-united-kingdom-2023/chapter-14-the-food-chai

28   https://researchbriefings.files.parliament.uk/documents/CBP-9665/CBP-9665.pdf

water companies to spill, destroying the ecology of whichever water body they're discharging into, which might be a river and is likely to be the property of a large landowner. Riparian ownership – if a water course runs 'through, beneath or adjacent' to your land – comes with rights and responsibilities. The main responsibilities include allowing the water to run freely, controlling any invasive species or maintaining assets, such as culverts or weirs, but if you're a landowner, you have the right to protect your property from flooding and for the water to flow in its 'natural quantity and quality'.

As ever, there are many good, responsible 'riparian owners', who seek consent or support for activity, want to improve and manage the quality or quantity of water for themselves, the environment and their community. These are usually small businesses and homeowners, but the abuses clearly far outweigh any success stories. For 'industry', the legal requirement falls on everyone and no one. A voluntary incentives-based system of regulation, tilted to favour "growth" over environmental outcomes, and the sacred, essential, underpinning role of private property ensures no meaningful change.

The Solutions

The common sense of today does not obviously lend itself to thinking in systemic, nuanced, liberatory terms about these issues. To do that requires a political strategy, which can translate the problems outlined above into winnable demands made by an appropriate political subject. There must also be a sense of interconnectedness that is built into any programme or campaign, which is difficult to do when so many of the working class has very little instinctive connection to the natural environment.

Many environmental workers already have this instinctive connection and think in systemic, nuanced terms. Many others don't. Many of them are anxious about the effect of the changing climate. For some, it's just a job and it fulfils other things that are more important to them, which the austerity-brained climate-reductionism of the employer favours. Fewer still perceive these issues in class terms. Nevertheless, a high degree of voluntarism exists in the environmental regulator: the workers are awake to the consequences of climate change and environmental degradation, which to greater and lesser degrees, cuts across the class divides and can be mobilising. In respect to water, it is just another catastrophic ecological situation in a litany of other catastrophic ecological situations. There remains a need, as always, to connect these political issues to 'bread-and-butter' demands. However, in the environmental regulator, these demands take on a different form because there is a direct connection between effective climate and environmental action and adequate resourcing. The unions aren't currently geared up to wage a campaign of this type. However, there is increasing rank-and-file activity in the regulator which is linking arms with the Unison rank and file movement 'Time for Real Change'.[29] And contrary to its self-perception, there is a higher-than-average capacity for spontaneous rank-and-file militancy. In the last decade, there have been two occasions when trade union members took unofficial, unreported industrial action, which pushed the organisation and the respective unions into unchartered territory, and even forced some concessions. However, these mini rebellions were defensive and limited to individual bread-and-butter issues. In other words, they did not seek to fundamentally change wider systems in the unions or the workplace.

Nevertheless, all of this demonstrates that there is a latent capacity for something more ambitious than the annual cycle of pay negotiations which dominates official union business. Lay activists, who have experimented with re-democratising their Unison branches and introducing more overtly political campaigns, report that this has a galvanising effect on members. One branch proudly reports full shop steward coverage at every major site within their area and has adopted the slogan 'Fighting for members and the environment,' which they believe reflects a genuine trend within the branch and the broader union. The potential of an ambitious campaign with an ecosocialist flavour cannot be guaranteed, because it has never been tested at any scale. But many activists would agree that the passions of environmental regulators and the 'anarchic' aspect to their character could be a good starting point.

Any such campaign, however, must develop beyond unions and isolated employers. The devastating consequences of not having an effective environmental regulator and responder finds its latest expression in the surface water flooding of Valencia, Spain. There, villages on the near-peripheral hinterland were devastated by torrential rain hitting land scorched by the earth from consecutive years of drought, leading to flooding which has killed 150+ people and brought about a simmering new, still unfolding, political crisis. This is not something we should hope to see replicated in England to provoke effective action. But with Labour threatening to cut the floods budget, this is a possibility communists and militants must be politically prepared for.[30] Communities at risk of flooding from rivers and sea are very aware of what flooding means.

---

29   https://timeforrealchange.uk/

30   Since this article has been drafted and published, a number of storms have battered Britain, causing flooding, destruction of infrastructure, farmland, homes and deaths.

They know what budget cuts can equate to, and they are often sympathetic to workers in this field, even if they reject their employer.

To store and capture water or protect communities and vital resources (such as domestic food production) against water, requires expertise. It also requires a state-like actor, which can command and coordinate: to transfer water, improve the health of water, bring salmon and invertebrates back to our water, and crack down on greedy polluters. What that body looks like and how it operates is worth deep consideration. At a minimum, it must be based on democratic forms which include communities and environmental workers.

Necessarily, land reform must feature as part of any future strategy which deals with the social realities of the ruralities. It is not unusual to drive through a rural market town and see a regional National Farmers Union (NFU) office standing out against a backdrop of dead, over-farmed land or the lonely decay of the high street. But while the NFU or the Country, Land and Business Association are hegemonic, they are far from universally popular, especially amongst small agriculturalists. Propertied rural reactionaries are finding other outlets for their expression, in campaigns which aim to pressure the traditional institutions and push them in new proto-fascistic directions.[31] Others – a distinct minority – reject them both and might be worked with. However, we shouldn't have any romantic notions about small landowners or tenanted farmers, as many feel aggrieved for being excluded from this elite group of property owners. This includes some tenant farmers, who could be predatory land monopolists themselves and exploit masses of cheap, foreign labour.[32] But it's plain that any mature campaign cannot neglect them, even just for the fact that rural propertied classes have made the downfall of many a revolution.

The unifying factor is the tremendously authoritarian and impersonal quality of private property relations, which forcibly organise, exploit and dominate people and the environment. Whether that be through parasitic outsourced companies, who prey on dysfunction to extract maximum profits; or, concentrations of corporate battery farms obliterating the health of rivers. Or, further still, it is the very personal, direct domination that water workers must bear witness to, or which farmworkers are subjected to in poly-tunnels, on yards and in fields, up and down the country. It is even frequently flooded communities, who can't get home insurance, can't move house and are kept awake at night when they hear rain start to fall.

---

31   https://x.com/NoFarmsNoFoods

32   https://notesfrombelow.org/article/workers-inquiry-seasonal-agricultural-labour-uk-sh

These experiences have a shared basis which could form the foundations of a political coalition with the capacity to transform the situation. Within the regulator, this must start with a campaign which links climate change and environmental degradation to resources and pay. These workers have a privileged position, in-part based on their essential function, which comes with responsibility and expectations. They are well positioned to be the central organising force that unifies the varied aims of these seemingly disparate groups into a coherent and forward-facing campaign. To do so is no small feat, but the moment demands it and if they don't, they must ask themselves: *did we do everything that we could possibly do?*

Something in the water

An anonymous water worker

For the past couple of years the water industry is enjoying a rare glimpse in the limelight. Although clearly it's for all the wrong reasons. This behemoth of an industry has been quietly working away in the background, in the shadows, seamlessly delivering potable water and taking away the sewage. It's not a sexy industry, and many would say it's taken for granted. But this laissez faire attitude is a key component in the mess that we're currently in. The industry has for too long been forgotten and been left to its own devices, with the consequences which are finally comping into light tofor the general public.

The financial shenanigans have been extensively documented in the mainstream press, with the byzantine financial corporate structures, siphoning of profits and bumper executive bonuses. But what do you know about the workers – the ones who actually toil day in day out and live with the consequences of a mismanaged industry that everyone has forgotten about? Fergal Sharkey likes to make the distinction between the Environment Agency bosses – who are in it for their bonus or political gain – and the workers, dedicated environmentalists who strive to improve the environment. The same analogy applies to the water industry. People don't come into this sector looking for bags of money or a high octane life. People are drawn to it from the sense of purpose they get forin delivering a basic human right – the access to safe water and sanitation. 35 years of privatisation has hardly eroded the sense of satisfaction of delivering a public good to your local community, although this has long been forgotten amongst the water sector boards and higher echelons. Like so many public sector jobs, the water industry tends to be a vocational sector where people find jobs for life, often having entire families and multiple generations working in the same company.

The water industry as a whole is faced with two key challenges: finances and sewage spills. Although these are inextricably related, they affect workers in different ways. The speculation around the future of Thames Water, and by extension the other large water firms, has resulted in a panicked tightening of the belt across the industry. With the main costs of these companies being energy, chemicals and payroll, capitalism obliges the first two to get paid unquestioned. As ever the pinch is felt by the little people who actually keep these places running. Terms and conditions across the sector have progressively worsened. You name it, the industry has done it: outsourcing, offshoring, lower than inflation pay rises, worsening pension provisions, changes to working patterns to include weekend work at no extra cost, reducing staff numbers with no reduction in workloads. It truly reads like a Dummy's Guide to Bad Practices. And yet these squeezed workers remain loyal to their duty to their communities, running on goodwill and essentially keeping the industry from completely collapsing.

Which brings us to the second point – sewage spills. And although sewage is in the media, the same issues apply to the treatment of potable water, with potentially even more serious implications. The asset stripping and siphoning of profits for shareholder dividends which has gone on for decades, when nobody was looking in the direction of the water companies, has left the entire asset base on its knees. Like all large infrastructure sectors the industry has large, costly assets that require constant maintenance and periodic renewal – all on a herculean scale. So clearly wWith no strong regulatory drive, the owners have preferred a light touch approach, spending little and pocketing big. But clearly this is completely unsustainable. And so we get to the present day – a skeleton crew of workers desperately trying to keep ageing assets working, sites that can only deliver a fraction of their design capacity, and bosses in denial about how we've ended up here.

Every worker that I have ever met in this industry comes to work every day looking to do a good job – the best they can even. The pride of working in this industry – until a couple of years ago at least – was a huge part of keeping things running smoothly. It's their passion, effort and willingness to go above and beyond that has saved the bacon of the company bosses. Operatives work extremely hard in difficult conditions because they care about their work and they care about the environment. The news reports around sewage spills can really feel like a punch in the gut for the workers who put so much into what they do. They would go into great details to outline the differences between raw sewage spills, consent breaches, storm discharges. Each is different and has a different impact on the receiving watercourse. They would also point out to the thriving biology in certain rivers, which can often improve after discharge points. They would reel off the numerous rivers where salmon and other fragile species have returned after decades of absence. And they would say all of this from sheer passion and devotion to the good work they do and their passion for the environment.

Which is absolutely not to say that companies should be let off the hook for the crisis we are seeing in our waterways. As often happens the lines are blurred – the industry as a whole is tarred but the real problem is the systemic mis management, not the devotion of the workers. The under investment in assets is real – and was a deliberate choice of company owners, present and past. The fact that companies take their operating licences for granted and believe they are untouchable is a genuine issue. The press are absolutely right to print story after story on the matter. But employee goodwill has been abused to the extent that the workers are doing the companies lobbying for them.

Some of the biggest opponents of renationalisation – or any version of a change in industry ownership model – is most vehemently opposed by the industry workers themselves, seemingly affected by some weird Stockholm Syndrome. It's true that renationalisation will not solve all of the problems – the nationalised model of Scotland and the not for profit model of Wales shows us that the industry issues affect those areas just as much as they do English water companies. But it must be better to allow profits to get reinvested rather thatn diverted to further bolster already deep capitalist pockets. The recent bailout package that is about to be handed to Thames Water to save them from complete collapse feels like a missed opportunity to discuss the bigger issues around alternative ownership models. Pumping further cash into the industry without seizing the opportunity for a systemic review of the way it is funded surely equates to kicking the can down the road.

Direniş means resistance: The strike of the Soma coal miners

Özay and Erdinç

A generation ago, the residents of the Soma valley supported themselves through subsistence agriculture and peasant smallholding. Now, they mine lignite - a low grade form of coal made up of compressed peat. The population of the district is just over 100,000 people, spread across the town of Soma and a collection of agricultural villages. Of that 100,000, 15% work in the five big mineworks. The Soma collieries sit amongst the hills of Western Turkey, a few hours' drive north from the coastal city of İzmir. The valleys around them used to be full of Tobacco plants, but now they are full of smoke. Lignite is the dirtiest form of coal and contains contaminants like Sulphur that cause deadly air pollution when burnt. The mining industry here was supercharged by the 'rush for coal' subsidy programme initiated by Erdogan's ruling Justice and Development Party (AKP) in 2012.[33] Natural gas imports from Iran and Russia led to a major current account deficit, so the AKP government aimed to replace them with domestic alternatives. In 2013, coal made up 25.8% of the Turkish grid's coal mix, and most of it was imported. In 2023, coal had grown to 36.2% of the fuel mix, and most of it is domestic lignite.[34] In Soma, the mined lignite is moved just a few miles to be burnt in the two local coal fired power plants before electricity flows into the grid along high voltage power lines towards Istanbul, İzmir and Ankara. This recomposition of the energy infrastructure wasn't a peaceful transition. The price of coal is death.

In 2014, 301 miners died in the Soma mine disaster. A fire started deep underground in the Eyne mine during a shift change. Despite other miners forming rescue teams and trying to save them, nearly half of the workers who were underground when the fire started never returned to the surface. It was the worst

---

33   Coşku Çelik, 'Extractivism and Labour Control: Reflections of Turkey's "Coal Rush" in Local Labour Regimes', Critical Sociology 49, no. 1 (1 January 2023): 59–76, https://doi.org/10.1177/08969205211046287.

34   'Türkiye Electricity Review 2024', Ember Energy, accessed 25 November 2024, https://ember-energy.org/latest-insights/turkiye-electricity-review-2024.

mine disaster in Turkish history, and it was directly caused by the drive to increase production and reduce safety standards that was associated with the rush for coal.[35]

Despite this, the AKP maintained strong support locally. The combination of neoliberal reform that destroyed state support for agriculture and the massive waves of migration associated with the forced relocation of Kurdish populations and Syrian refugees has produced a new rural proletariat in valleys like this – and it is a proletariat that is entirely reliant on state-backed extractive industries. Without coal, they would have nothing.[36]

But despite this reliance, the deaths of the 301 planted seeds. Ever since then, a new union has been germinating underground, amongst the lignite. This independent union, the Bağımsız Maden İşçileri Sendikası, has grown slowly to become a union capable of taking on the mine bosses and winning.
Notes From Below spoke to two miners from the independent miners' union who had recently participated in a 54-day strike. The conversation was made possible by Umut-Sen, an independent workers' project that aims to support the class struggle across a range of industries including mining, warehousing, food delivery and office work. They set up a meeting between NFB and the Soma miners, then acted as translators and facilitators of the discussion that followed.
—

When they talk about their struggle, Erdinç and Özay always use a particular word: direniş. Our translators render it as 'resistance'. Rather than joining the union and going on strike, the miners talk about joining the resistance and starting to resist. At the end of the interview, we ask them why they use this specific term. "Direniş is not like a protest," Erdinç clarifies, "it is active and direct. You use your teeth and your bones."

Erdinç started working in the mines in 2003. He went deep underground in the lignite seams of Soma as a mechanic. His role was to prevent flooding by maintaining water pumps, checking water levels, and carrying out repairs on any faults in the pumping

35   Fikret Adaman, Murat Arsel, and Bengi Akbulut, 'Neoliberal Developmentalism, Authoritarian Populism, and Extractivism in the Countryside: The Soma Mining Disaster in Turkey', The Journal of Peasant Studies 46, no. 3 (16 April 2019): 514–36, https://doi.org/10.1080/03066150.2018.1515737. Coşku Çelik, 'Extractivism and Labour Control: Reflections of Turkey's "Coal Rush" in Local Labour Regimes', Critical Sociology 49, no. 1 (1 January 2023): 59–76

36   E. Irem Az, 'Against Exploitation and Contempt', 1+1 Express, 30 June 2019, https://birartibir.org/against-exploitation-and-contempt/; Coşku Çelik, 'The Making of the Rural Proletariat in Rural Turkey', in The Condition of the Working Class in Turkey: Labour under Neoliberal Authoritarianism, ed. Çağatay Edgücan Şahin and Mehmet Erman Erol (Place of publication not identified: Pluto Press, 2021).

system. After twenty years in the mines, he had gained a lot of experience. That matters, he says, because experience teaches you how to keep yourself and your colleagues safe.

Özay started working in the mines in 2007. He is a chemical technician. In practice, that means he tried to keep the tunnels sealed, finding the cracks where water was flowing into the mine and plugging them. It is a skilled job - so skilled that even the companies who make the products Özay uses couldn't repeat what he does, says Erdinç. It's also a notoriously dangerous role.

Their description of their work doesn't do justice to what the labour process looks like to the untrained eye. In a video shared by the independent miners' union (Bağımsız Maden İşçileri Sendikası) that shows the conditions underground, workers wade through tunnels in murky water up to their chests. Streams of water pour in from fault lines on the walls as technicians working by the light of their head torches desperately try to get the situation under control.

In August 2024, Erdinç and Özay were both working for Fernas Mining, a company owned by Ferhat Nasıroğlu, an AKP MP. Fernas is notorious in Soma for its working conditions.

"It is full of stress and mobbing [bullying]," Özay says. "We went to work one hour earlier than everyone else and went home two hours later. We wore our own clothes in the mine because we weren't given any protective equipment. The food they gave us was inedible, and the technicians I worked alongside have not had any of the proper training – they know about geology, not mining. On the weekends we were forced to work extra days for free. The wages are less than other mines, as well."

"I find it shameful to talk about, because I worked in these conditions for five years before I did anything about it."

In the Fernas mines there are 4 shifts of 70 production workers. Of that 70, 60 are underground at any one time. In addition to these 280 production workers, there were another 150 office and support workers, making a total of 430.

Given the near total absence of safety regulation, inspection and enforcement, accidents are inevitable. The mines are deadly workplaces, and everyone involved knows it. Özay and Erdinç were both working in 2014 when the 301 died. Özay survived because he wasn't working underground that day. Erdinç was part of the search and rescue effort that tried to save any fellow workers left alive. The disaster brought attention to the complete failure of safety inspections in the mines and the awful conditions facing the workforce – for a moment, at least. After the disaster, wages rose and working hours fell.

It was after the 301 died that the union formed. 400m underground, a group of workers met to discuss their situation. In the mines, they couldn't be observed as closely, and they used that freedom to begin to organise. In most collieries they have to struggle against the 'triangle' of the state, the company, and the yellow union. Many workplaces have representatives from one of the 'ideologically compatible' corporatist union federations who maintain a hold over the workforce through ethnic affinity networks, rigged ballots and physical intimidation.[37]

For years, the independent union had been growing at Fernas, as workers began to organise against the terrible conditions they faced. Erdinç became a shop

---

37   Çağatay Edgücan Şahin, 'Organised Workers' Struggles under Neoliberalism: Unions, Capital and the State in Turkey', in The Condition of the Working Class in Turkey: Labour under Neoliberal Authoritarianism, ed. Çağatay Edgücan Şahin and Mehmet Erman Erol (Place of publication not identified: Pluto Press, 2021).

steward in 2020, after seeing how the independent union fought for the 8,000 miners in Soma who had been promised compensation but never paid it. He was recruited by the late president of the union, Tahir Çetin.[38] Özay's conditions as a chemical technician were more comfortable than those of his friends in the mine, but he felt responsible – he had to fight with them. "I joined the resistance. My family were very proud of me for joining, as were my friends. It was honour that made me join."

Fernas management were increasingly aware of the growing union presence. Unlike other mines, they didn't have a sweetheart deal with a corporatist union set up to block independent organisation. So, they used another tactic: they victimised two union members, firing them on the spot. But that wasn't the end of it. The next day, after he had just worked a night shift, HR called Erdinç into a meeting. They sat there with the managers and fired him too.

"I warned them," he says, "I warned them that my union will stand beside me. But they didn't care." He was wearing a smart watch, and quietly began recording the meeting.

The union mobilised rapidly. The union president, lawyer, and other representatives all demanded to speak to management. For ten days, they were ignored. On the 24th of August they started their strike. They set up pickets in front of the mine, and 120 of the 280 production workers joined them. It was a minority strike from the start. From the first day of picketing, the police were a key factor.

"70 people were taken into custody on the first day. The police kept them overnight and released them the next morning. When they were released, they came straight back to the picket line."

The union understood that they couldn't win the strike only by picketing the mine, so they did some research and found that Fernas also owns a luxury hotel in the costal town of Bodrum. "We started protesting there, and we gained huge popularity with the people of Bodrum." But the police repression didn't let up. "Some of us were detained by the police in Bodrum again, 3 or 4 times, and in Soma there were also 2 more lots of detentions."

---

38   Halil Burak, 'The Fig Pierces the Rock, the Ship Overcomes the Water', 1+1 Express, 30 June 2019, https://birartibir.org/the-fig-pierces-the-rock-the-ship-overcomes-the-water/; Avci Bekir, 'A Union Governed by Those Who Produce', 1+1 Express, 5 January 2020, https://birartibir.org/a-union-governed-by-those-who-produce/.

We ask if this was the kind of police repression that they expected at the start of the strike. Our translators clarify, yes, this is the general procedure against any protest. What happened when they were detained?

"They interrogate us, they ask us questions, and we give our side. Sometimes people are beaten. We do health checks. Then we get released. It takes 10-12 hours."

At this point, the strike had shrunk to 80 people. They had a meeting and decided what to do next. They would divide their forces: 35 people in front of the mine in Soma, 5 people in front of the hotel in Bodrum, 5 people in Istanbul, and 35 people would go to the capital, Ankara.

Erdinç and Özay were both in the Ankara delegation. They went to the Fernas headquarters and protested there for three days. Once again, they were detained. Erdinç himself was detained four times during the strike.

"There wasn't so much violence," he says, "some people did receive a beating and they objected – they said we are not terrorists, why are you doing this? The police said, 'We are only doing our job.'"

After this round of detentions, the strikers headed back to Soma for another meeting. They decided to give the company five days to settle the strike, or else they would begin to march from Soma to Ankara. The company responded by sending the police to detain the union president. He was held for two days. During his detention the rest of the strikers prepared to march. When he was released, they set off.

They marched without shoes, covering 180 miles in seven days. They used buses for any roads which were unsafe to walk along. Finally, they arrived at the edge of Ankara. By this time, the struggle had begun to gain national prominence. Ferhat Nasıroğlu, the owner of Fernas and AKP MP, had been using his platform in parliament to lie about the miners and spread propaganda against them. "He said we had been brainwashed by the far left," Erdinç says, laughing. So, when they finally arrived in the city, they went straight to the parliament building. Supportive MPs invited them inside, and they marched in, barefoot.

Every night, they camped in Salvation Park, and every day, they protested at parliament. They weren't making any progress, so they decided to march to the Ministry of Labour, only to be stopped by the police. "We were so angry.

When they stopped us, we made a decision: we will go on hunger strike. We sat down then and there, all of us, even the union lawyer."

The next day the police detained them yet again and tried to force them to eat, but it didn't work. On the 12th day of hunger strike, they decided to take a collective vow of silence. "We asked the people to speak for us." 40 spontaneous protests began in 18 different cities across Turkey, with people taking to the street to be their voice against the police and the company.

Then, finally, on the 54th day of the strike, they heard that the company had agreed to begin negotiations. "It was midnight when we heard. We were very happy. We drank soup that night, and everybody was very emotional. The next day we returned to Soma. When we left Ankara, there were many supporters to see us off. Even the police said they were happy that we had won."

"For 25 days since we left Soma we had not seen our families. We were happy to go home. We spent three hours with them the next morning, then met back in front of the mine to begin negotiations. It took three days." Fernas folded completely, granting the union 95% of its demands. "We won promotions, bonuses, salaries, better working conditions, health and safety…" Erdinç trails off, seemingly still amazed by the scale of their victory.

What would they say to workers in Britain?

"You must be together. On our way to Ankara, we shared our problems with each other, we united with each other and became one."

"For workers in Britain – if you go on strike as 30 people, do not think of yourself as 30 people. Not even one person should think about what would happen to them alone. You should all think about what happens to you collectively. What will it be like to win, to win together? To win by fighting? Those are the questions you should ask."

Erdinç and Özay have not returned to work. They were two of the three people fired by management at the end of the strike. Now they work in an olive oil factory nearby. The union found them these jobs: the other members view it as their responsibility to look after comrades who have been victimised. They spend their days lugging 50kg barrels of oil back and forth and managing the extraction process. It's hard manual work, but less dangerous than going underground.

Despite their victimisation, they are proud. "We couldn't go back to our jobs. But we won something big and important for everyone else. It is our pride, our honour to have contributed to such a big victory for our friends."
"Nobody should be in the hands of the rich." Özay emphasises this. "If I only looked after my own comfort, I wouldn't have lost my job. But I am very happy that I did, because my friends have kept their jobs, and they have won. I would rather have been the 302nd to die in the disaster than carry on working in those conditions and do nothing."

Update from Umut-Sen, 7.12.2024

Something impressive happened today that we wanted to share. At Polonez Gıda (an Istanbul sausage factory) the bosses were uncomfortable with union mobilization and fired 13 workers. In response, the workers who wanted their friends back began a direniş inside the factory, while the union posted a strike decision. The workers' struggle has been ongoing for about 140 days now.

The workers suffer from problems such as heavy working conditions, long shifts, overtime, and low wages. Yesterday, they made a statement: "We have shared our problems with all state institutions but could not find a solution. We are marching to Ankara as a last resort. We call on everyone to support our Constitutional Rights March." This scenario is, of course, reminiscent of the Fernas miners. Similarly, and unfortunately, they were attacked and prevented by the police. They stated that they would start a hunger strike today.

The key point we want to emphasize is that workers are carefully observing each other's experiences, quickly learning and adopting each other's methods and means of struggle. If Fernas workers had not previously resorted to these struggle tactics, Polonez food workers would probably not have adopted this approach.

Power Systems and Renewables

In the interview below, NFB speaks with B, a Senior Power Systems Engineer. B discusses the dynamics of digital modelling on the UK power grid; the future impacts and implications of the green energy transition on contemporary workforces; and the wider infrastructural problems emerging from the growing reliance on the renewable energy sector.

Could you talk a bit about your work on renewables and the UK power grid?

I'm a Senior Power Systems Engineer. I work with energy developers seeking to build solar generators or wind farms, especially in the UK. I do a lot of digital modelling, looking at different situations, and seeing what would happen in various scenarios. My main job involves enabling companies who are developing renewable energy plants to maximise efficiency in generating and transmitting energy to customers.

The power grid is a very dynamic system, yet the UK's capacity for new renewable energy connections is quite low. You can think of the power grid like a series of pipes that the power flows through like water. The thing is, at every single moment, the demand must exactly match the generation, because there is minimal storage. Whereas the plumbing system stores water as well as transports it, the power system does not. So, every single moment, generators are responding to changes in demand. These are easier to predict over an aggregate country, and much harder to predict over a household, because the generator is completely blind as to whether or not you turn on your lights at any given moment. But it can look at the average time people turn on their lights, and react according to that prediction.

In most countries, we distinguish between transmission and distribution. Generally, it's based on voltage. Think of high voltage power lines, long distances, a lot of energy – that's transmission. Distribution is getting energy from the transmission grid to your house. In some countries the distribution operator also sells the energy to households. Whereas in other countries that task is performed by independent companies. Which is why, for example, in Ireland, you can buy your energy from whichever company, but it's coming from the same lines.

We have this challenge that's been growing in recent years, with very aggressive renewable energy targets that have been set in most of Europe. You end up facing a really big challenge, which is demand response matching: this gets harder when you add distance and variability. What I mean by that is you can put a natural gas power plant in the centre of London, and it can serve London immediately. You have an adjustable knob on it and you can say exactly how much power you want to output at any second to match the demand in London. Whereas when you want to serve London via wind or via solar, you lose two critical things. First, you lose this adjustable knob, because you don't control when the sun is out and you don't control when the wind is blowing, and that might not line up with when people are using power. You also lose the choice of location, so now you might have to transmit over a long distance. There aren't giant wind farms and there aren't giant solar farms in the centre of London. There are a few rooftop ones, but they are not serving the vast majority of the demand.

We might see, for example, that there are wind farms in Scotland, and their power is being sent down to England. Now, when you're sending it over long distances, suddenly it matters a lot that you don't have enough capacity on your lines. If you think of them as pipes, they can't hold any more water, and you can't transmit any more power on that line. So your options are to build new lines, to build closer power plants, or use that old natural gas plant that we already have in the centre of London.

The general public are very resistant to new power lines. What ends up happening is that a lot of those windfarms in Scotland, when there isn't enough room on the power lines, end up getting shut off: because there simply isn't enough space on the lines to take that power where it needs to go. So even though there is loads of excess energy, it's not where the customers are, and it's not when the customers need it. This is a huge problem that has fundamentally shifted the power grid infrastructure in the last ten-twenty years.

If you are a wind or solar developer, and you get shut off, you're usually not gonna get paid for energy that does not get sold to a customer. This is what we call curtailment, and it's pretty massive. And the visibility on that, for renewable energy developers, is pretty low. So one of the things that I often look at is strategic placement of new generators to avoid as much curtailment as possible. I simulate the grid under different conditions to estimate how much they would get curtailed, and then they can make their business decisions off of that.

Day-to-day, what does your job involve?

We get a lot of very varied inquiries from developers, asking can I do this, can I do that. And we don't always have a set up for that process. So I do a lot of the key development of the new processes. Whereas some of my fellow engineers would be running studies and simulations – I do a lot of work to automate the steps of those studies. So I have to do a lot of research, and a lot of data exploration and manipulation. Most of what we do is based on publicly available data. The UK publishes almost all of their power grid data (some countries publish nothing), so there's a huge amount of data out there, and I spend a lot of time working with it. That means some excel use, but mainly I do python automation.[39]

I develop python scripts that run these power system studies, with interfaces designed for an experienced engineer to utilise. The scripts include data interpretation to bring together disparate data sources and set up a model to simulate power flow. Then, after running the simulations, they clean up the results and process them into digestible reports and charts that our customers can understand, since most of our customers are not engineers themselves, but sales teams and decision makers for developers.

I work in the office three days a week, and then from home for two. That's kind of the standard. And that's what I wanted, because my previous job was fully remote, and I was a bit miserable. I am around co-workers a lot, although it's not super collaborative. There are moments of collaboration, and all of our code gets reviewed by each other. It's a very small company, so it's very tight-knit, and we do an impressive amount for the size of our company. We run 150-ish reports a year for renewable developers in the UK.

What other factors do you have to consider in setting up something like a solar plant?

We consider a lot of things. Something that's quite UK-specific is the 'queue'. Under previous UK law - this has recently changed but we're still dealing with the relics of it - you could submit a speculative application to connect to the grid even if you had no intention of building a power plant. Even if you didn't have planning permission, you could just submit as many speculative applications as you wanted. What that resulted in is what we call the 'queue' – a ranked list, first-come-first-serve.

---

39   Python is a computer programming language.

So, if you applied ten years ago to build a 100 megawatt solar farm in England, then you are high on the list, and we would have to consider everyone after you as being curtailed, because you won't be, right? So if there wasn't enough room on the power lines, you would get priority. The problem is that over many years, hundreds (if not thousands) of completely speculative applications for projects that will never be built have clogged up the queue. So now developers are told there is no room, because of people in line ahead of you. Many don't actually intend to build their projects, or can't build these. Some are genuine. A lot of the time they will apply for four different projects, with the intention of only building one. They want to see which one has the best finances, the best whatever, before they build it. But those three other projects stay in the queue.

Measures have been introduced to check developers are making steps towards their projects, and to remove projects that aren't going forward. But there is still a lot of legacy stuff clogging it, and preventing development, because the distribution and transmission operators tell the renewable developers that there's no room and that they can't build. But they might actually want to, whereas the people in line ahead of them aren't going to.

What are the main renewables in the UK and Ireland?

Definitely wind and solar. In the UK, you would see solar more common in England, and wind more common north of England. It's as simple as that for the most part. In Ireland, it's more wind. Each country has its own profile, its own characteristics, and its own unique problems. Germany, for example, has a problem very similar to the UK, where they have all their wind power in the north, and high demand for electricity consumption in the south. So you have the same transmission constraint issue.

Solar has its own problem: it turns off really fast. You could have 100 gigawatts of solar producing energy in your country, but the sun sets quite fast. In that time, how do you ramp up? Because demand doesn't actually fall when the sun goes down. In most situations it goes up, because people are turning on their lights, going home, etc. In California, we call it the 'duck curve': a curve that expresses the disparity between when solar goes offline, and when demand is needed.

It's a huge problem, because if there's no storage in the system, and generators have to match demand every single millisecond of every day, then what happens is you have to ramp up your fossil fuel generators, or your batteries (if you have batteries, which most places don't) so fast. Sometimes it goes beyond the physical capability of the generator. This is a huge issue, and causes a lot of power quality issues, instability, and outages.

There are troubles everywhere. Renewables is a quickly changing space. Previously, it was stagnant for so long. Imagine if the national plumbing network suddenly had a different option besides water, and you had to manage that. It's crazy. It's a huge shift, but it's definitely doable. Researchers have proven this time and time again. It's a matter of prioritisation and government resources. And not just in renewables, but also power lines: which is difficult, because there is huge resistance to them. People want to bury them underground. But that costs ten times as much. And if you're pulling power lines from Scotland to London, ten times as much is a lot more for 1,000km than it is for 10km. Really, there isn't an alternative way to move the energy, because London needs power. And you can't build a giant wind farm, or a solar farm, in London city. There isn't space for it. You can only build it outside of it. So you still need to get the power in, via whatever line you can manage.

It's not easy to build new infrastructure. Building overhead lines is so much easier, and faster, but people don't like them. In my opinion, the Conservative Party sometimes push for lines to be undergrounded, partly because they know that it will drive up the cost of renewable energy, and make it look like a worse idea. They'll say - look how expensive this renewable transition is. But they'll also be agitating for underground lines. There's a way to make this cheaper, but they don't like it.

With the decline of fossil-fuel plants, there are campaigns around 'just transition', keeping current workforces employed in renewable energy. There are tensions around this, transitioning without devastating communities reliant upon existing energy industries. How do you see these tensions playing out as renewables grow?

I think it is going to be very difficult. Especially because, although the skills are transferable, it's not the same type of job. Working in an oil refinery you have hundreds, if not thousands, of employees, who are coming to the same place every day. Whereas renewable energy, once constructed, employs remarkably few people. A massive solar farm might employ ten people a year: to come and clean it, to maintain it, to take care of the metres. But the bulk job would be the building. This would be a very different type of work than what workers in these industries are maybe used to, which in most cases would be a stable, one-location job. Instead, you'd be trucking around the country, and having a different job every six months.

So, it's a huge shift in the worker culture. I don't know about the union status of it, cause again that's more like the workers on the ground building, maintaining and operating all that stuff. It's definitely a challenge, and there needs to be options for people leaving that space, something that should be addressed by governments pushing this transition forwards. These things need to be built, and we need workers to build them. But after they are built, those jobs dry up. There should be greater efforts to work on not just transitioning people from gas to wind, but also out of the industry. Because it will shrink.

There's a lot of daily maintenance that goes into managing fossil fuel generators, so the employee count is pretty significant. In my opinion, I don't see the entire thing going away. Oil refineries, for example, also make plastics, they make a lot of the stuff we use in our daily lives. And even if we were to stop burning oil, or coal, or natural gas, we're not giving up plastics. We're not making great strides in that direction, currently.

Is there a trade-union that represents workers in your specific workplace or wider sector?

I'm not in one, and I don't know if there is one that would represent my sector. But, it doesn't mean I'm not up for it. I think it's important for long term security. Our company is small now, but it could grow. And if it were to grow, there would be a greater disconnect between the employees and the CEO, who can't personally know everyone forever if it were to grow. So I feel it would be a long term protection against potential problems, and better to start it now so it's there when you need it, even if we don't need that now. As far as the rest of the industry goes, I'm not sure if there is a union. I've never looked it up, but I really should! Part of it, I think, is that I'm from the US, and trade-unions aren't exactly ingrained in our culture. I've never been approached by anyone about a trade-union, or offered to join a trade-union. So I don't know if any place I've ever worked has had one.

Considering your current work on the UK power grid, is there anything in particular that marks the industry as standing out more than other countries?

It's pretty typical, although there's this massive burden being placed upon Scotland: bearing the brunt of hosting and transmitting power to England. I think that is fascinating given the historical context of the relationship between these countries. A lot of Scottish people might not feel that great about building loads of transmission lines over their land, and lots of wind power on their land, to go sell to England, right? It's not really surprising that there would be a big resistance there. It is interesting how the natural environment kind of reinforces this historic contention. Wind power exists in Scotland, less so in England, so there is naturally a desire to use it for England. Otherwise, the dynamic of a load-heavy capital city that needs loads of power is not special. Paris is a huge load centre. Almost every country will have a huge load centre that has loads of power lines coming out of it to pull power from elsewhere.

So what we're seeing is the UK just trying to get power from anywhere. They are building lines anywhere they can, because they need power so bad, and they don't really have enough. The UK also has this peculiar phenomenon which isn't present in the rest of Europe. As I mentioned before, the generators and the load have to match at all times. And at 5pm sharp there's a huge spike in demand across the UK and Ireland that is really hard for generators to match. This is from people switching on their kettles.

Interestingly, Northern Ireland is completely run by the Irish operator. It's not really connected to or run by the UK at all. It's not in any of the UK datasets. It's completely left out. There are two or three HVDC (High Voltage Direct Current) links that connect Ireland to the UK. You could think of these as power without a frequency. So it's not a wave, it's a line. That means the grids aren't synchronised together. It's just a one-way flow of power. Those links connect the countries and, unsurprisingly, Ireland does a lot of power exporting to the UK.

During my masters, I modelled the European power grid as a whole, in high resolution. It was an intersectional kind of study, with law and international relations. I looked at the way renewable energy and grid efficiency can be improved by international cooperation - managing the grid together, rather than managing it as individual countries, which is predominately how it is currently managed. Efficiency is dramatically improved. The carbon emissions that are expected from an internationally managed grid are also far lower than our current system. The less carbon emissions, the less inefficiency. All of it.

This is mainly because of traverse flows. So, renewable solar energy in Spain could help Germany when their supply of wind is low. That is one example of collaboration that could improve the efficiency of the grid. If it currently happens, it's more or less by coincidence than by intention. The problem is that a lot of countries manage their cross-border flows in ways that can prevent that cooperation. You have countries turning down generators to respect cross-boundary limits. If those were adjusted more as a whole, rather than as a country, efficiency can be improved.

If you look at the open infrastructure map - https://openinframap.org/ - you can see a lot of stuff isn't really cross-border. Lots of power lines are very distinctly broken at borders. You shouldn't be able to see borders on this map, but you definitely can, showing the way the grid is managed is quite local.

What are the most important things you've learned about the structure of the energy industry, and what can we expect in coming years with the growth of renewables?

I think people don't know how it works, and lack of awareness causes a lot of problems. Especially when its policymakers writing about a system they don't understand. People in the sector then have to deal with that: whatever kind of nonsense has been put forward. For example, saying we would like to have 100% renewables by 2050. I personally think that's a great goal, but the practicality of it is a whole different question. The people who actually operate the grid are becoming more and more stressed, because it's getting harder with renewable energy to run it.

There's not really any discussion on what flexibility we're okay with. For example, power outages are seen as an absolute no, for good reason. People have medicines that have to be refrigerated, people have respirators at home in some situations. There's all kinds of reasons people shouldn't be losing power. But there isn't really any discussion on how prepared we are for a real outage. How prepared as a society are we for climate change causing these things to happen? Because if there was a giant power outage, people would blame renewables, not the policymakers who made it nearly impossible for the operators to run the grid.

I'm all for the energy transition. But we do have to discuss what we are willing to sacrifice. Are we willing to deal with a 1-5% lack of power, and with seasonal variability? If the answer is no, then we're putting ourselves in a pretty tight knot.

Are situations like mass power outages likely to accompany the transition to renewable power?

Absolutely. They already are. If you look at California, the power system is an absolute disaster. One major power company, PG&E, was found to be responsible for wildfires that destroyed cities. And so when the conditions for wildfires were very high, such as high temperatures and high winds, that power company opted to turn off their power for loads of customers. So a huge blackout ensued for extended periods, because that company was like - the risk of wildfires is too high, we're turning off our power. Then they can't be held liable for any wildfires that start. That was (understandably) not well received.

California is an incredibly interesting international case study on power grids. Another is the Texas power outage, which occurred during a snowstorm in February 2021. Renewable energy was blamed. Wind turbines shut off during the storms, and people were without power. But that wasn't because of the wind turbines: that was just a media presentation of what happened. The actual situation goes back to how the Texas power grid is set up. Texas has its own power grid, which avoids federal regulations for grids spanning multiple states. They have their own regulations, which have different standards, which cause their grid to be less stable, and it's more likely to fail - which it has, and will again.

Climate change is affecting places that are insecure to start with. This is all just giving us a window into the future. We can expect that in ten-to-twenty years time, many places will have devastating outages. I can't say that with 100% certainty, but this is my perspective. We need to be prepared and understand that partly these things are going to happen if we want to transition. We should be aware of and manage those risks ahead of time rather than acting surprised when they happen.

Feminist Co-Research: The case of retail workers in Slovenia

Ana Cvelfar, Živa Šketa and Marja Zakelšek

Ana Cvelfar, Živa Šketa and Marja Zakelšek are members of CEDRA (Centre for Social Research), a socialist organisation.

Introduction

CEDRA (Centre for Social Research) is a Slovenian organisation focused on organising workers at their workplace with the goal of building strong workers' organisations that will unite in a single socialist workers' movement. We understand organising for economic demands (improving workers' rights and working conditions in individual companies or sectors) as a lever for workers' politicisation. In this contribution, we will present an example of this approach: a feminist co-research in TUŠ, one of the retail companies in Slovenia. Our claim is that by entering the workplace and organising with workers to establish a union at TUŠ and through organising for better working conditions, we opened a terrain for political work with retail workers.

A brief history of CEDRA

CEDRA's history can be linked back to the popular uprisings throughout Slovenia between 2012 and 2014 as a response to the government's handling of the worsening economic crisis. A group of activists, students, and academics gathered around the informal group Delavsko-punkerska univerza and student party Iskra, articulated a desired alternative to the existing political establishment: democratic socialism – linking a socialist project with the strengthening of democratic procedures and gradual expansion of democracy from political to the economic sphere. In 2014, the political party Initiative for Democratic Socialism (IDS) was established. IDS formed the new-left coalition with two other recently established and loosely social-democratic parties and some civil-society movements. In the same year, they entered parliamentary politics as United Left (ZL). Soon, different factions began to emerge within IDS and ZL, with the main dispute revolving around the question of where to direct available funding and members' capacity: on the parallel grassroots movement, building the power of the trade unions and activist groups, or on strengthening the parliamentary party through 'parliamentary activities and sound PR strategy [which are] at least as important as building a grassroots movement, due to the enlarged potential to directly influence legislative procedures and shape public opinion.' The 'parliamentary orientation' prevailed within the party, and around two hundred founding IDS members left IDS (and the United Left) while publicly denouncing the undemocratic means with which the group focused on parliamentary politics consolidated the coalition into the Left party.[40]

CEDRA was established in 2016 by a small part of those who left IDS and recognised the failure of building a working-class base as the main reason for the failure of the democratic socialist project of IDS. The initial idea behind CEDRA was thus: rather than forming a political party with a socialist program and then bringing this program to the working class in the form of the party, we should first offer help with workers' organising in various sectors and form organic connections with workers. CEDRA drew on operaist theory, according to which political unity of the working class is not achieved automatically, and its form is never given once and for all. During Slovenia's transition from self-managed socialism to capitalism (from the early 1990s to 2004), the political composition of the working class was shaped by the form of the reformed trade unions, which managed to get significant concessions from the emerging national bourgeoisie. However, between 2004 and 2008 the conditions for the initial class compromise eroded significantly.[41] Collective bargaining at the sectoral level often seems to be limited to extending particular concessions to capital. At the company level, unions grew increasingly weak as well. Now, CEDRA views trade unions as an infrastructure we can use to enter the workplace. Only organising at the place of production allows us to recognise today's Slovenian working class, that is, the particular ways in which capital divides and manages workers to adjust labour power to the current requirements of accumulation, and search for a political form capable of breaking with the current technical composition of the labour force through challenges and successes in organising attempts.

---

40   This paragraph is a brief summary of the longer article written by ex-IDS members Furlan, S., Slukan, N. and Hergouth, M. in 2018. Their article *Maping Left Actors: Slovenia* is accessible at the following link: https://rosalux.rs/wp-content/uploads/2022/04/136_mapping_left_actors_slovenia_saso_furlan_et_al_rls_2018.pdf

41   For a more detailed analysis see: Bembič, Branko (2018): From victory to victory to the final retreat. Changing balance of class forces in the Slovenian transition. Tiempo devorado (Vol. 4, Issue 2, pp. 363–398). Universitat Autonoma de Barcelona.

Why organise the retail sector?

CEDRA started to work with workers' collectives and unions in manufacturing, education, journalism, care work, and the logistics union in seaport Luka Koper. Acting at first mainly through providing educational workshops for workers and union representatives, in that period, CEDRA helped to establish two unions in the care work sector: workers union in private dialysis centres *(Sindikat zdravstvenega in socialnega varstva Nefrodial)* and the union of personal assistants for people with disabilities *(Sindikat osebne asistence – SOA)*.

After this period of simultaneous organising attempts in various sectors, the decision was made to focus primarily on the retail sector. Reproduction of the labour force is happening 1) in households (unpaid labour-force, invisible work), 2) in the private sector and 3) in the public sector. Retail companies are one of the most important components for the reproduction of the working class in the private sector, as they sell food and other basic necessities. If the price of basic necessities falls, so does the price of labour in general, as workers can maintain a "decent standard of living" on nominally lower wages. In the retail sector, the main mechanism for ensuring cost competitiveness while retaining the same or an even higher share of surplus value is by lowering wages, increasing work intensity and introducing precarious forms of work[42]. So, on the one hand, we have workers in the retail sector who live on minimum wages and have health issues because of the intensity of work. On the other hand, we have workers in different sectors whose real wages are higher if the cost of basic necessities is lower. This contradiction becomes even more visible in the case of workers in the Slovenian export sector, which primarily exports to Germany and other countries of the capitalist core. Here, workers' wages are nominally lower than the wages of their German colleagues, but in the Slovenian context, those are high real wages because of the low costs of reproduction, which allows the Slovenian export sector cost competitiveness abroad. We can clearly see how this creates fragmentation of the labour force. Our strategy is to organise key sectors of reproduction, starting with retail, in order to break with the segmentation of the working class and establish the conditions for political unity.

---

[42]   On our website you can read articles discussing the intensification of labor in the translation of the first issue of our irregular journal *Class Issue:* https://www.cedra.si/razredni-broj/class-issue-eng/class-issue-1-the-intensification-of-labor-december-2023

This decision to focus on the retail sector came in 2021 after an extensive analysis of the retail sector in Slovenia. The decision was based primarily on co-research interviews conducted with workers in Lidl and Aldi (operating in Slovenia under the brand name Hofer) as well as two public campaigns in which CEDRA actively participated. First was the campaign to re-hire the Lidl workers' union president, whom Lidl fired after she successfully formed the first union in the company. The second campaign was for the complete closure of shops in Slovenia on Sundays and holidays. In this campaign, CEDRA worked with the sectoral retail union (SDTS), the Association of Free Trade Unions (ZSSS), and the Left party. After a successful campaign for Sunday closures, CEDRA gained the trust of the sectoral union which started to give CEDRA contacts of existing union members. We were given a free hand to contact them and try to strengthen unions by establishing shop-level workers committees. CEDRA also gained some modest but significant funding that allowed employment first of one and later two people to work full-time with those workers' committees.

In 2021, CEDRA's primary activity was to help the workers' union in Lidl survive. To achieve this, we had to strengthen an active union membership and gain as many new members as possible to make the existing members less vulnerable to the company's disciplinary measures. While the membership and activities of the workers' union in Lidl were rising, we managed to establish an active group chat in which the majority of union members participated. We started the union's Facebook page, writing posts about working conditions in Lidl with existing members, hoping relatable posts would encourage others to join the union. However, we failed to establish a collective decision-making structure inside the union, which resulted in the burden of responsibility and exposure hanging disproportionately on the shoulders of the union president. After constant disciplinary measures the company directed mainly against her, she left her job in Lidl and sought other employment, but was still serving as union president. With no existing member willing to take her place, the union became more passive, and the membership dropped.

The story was different with the union in the TUŠ, until recently a Slovenian-owned retail company. We helped establish this union in the middle of 2021 with just six active members. The union membership grew to around 500 members by the year 2024.[43] The process of building the union from the ground up was

---

43   You can read a detailed report on TUŠ union and all its successful campaigns on out website: https://www.cedra.si/en/our-three-year-struggle

similar to the one in Lidl: a group chat for all members, weekly meetings, and a Facebook page, with the difference that in TUŠ the collective decision-making structure came to life in the form of a workers committee, Red TUŠ (Rdeči TUŠ). Currently, around 50 TUŠ shops nationwide have at least one representative on this working committee. This representative is responsible for collecting grievances from co-workers in the shop where they work, discussing further actions of the union from the committee with their colleagues, and then reporting their colleagues' attitudes back to the committee. In the last two years, workers from the TUŠ workers committee started joining CEDRA and helping with organising other companies, mainly in Spar, and working more closely with other CEDRA activists, participating in co-research and preparing for the organising school. An active committee of TUŠ union also gave us the opportunity to start with the feminist co-research discussed in the next section.

Feminist co-research

The idea of a co-research project relating to women's oppression began at the end of 2022, when the TUŠ union experienced its first widespread wave of mobilisation due to dissatisfaction with working conditions. More and more TUŠ workers started to recognise the union as a structure through which they could address their grievances and demands. In December 2022, a mobilisation towards a strike started to materialise. This also implied the first serious possibility for CEDRA to start implementing wider political issues that concern the working class as a whole, to a broad group of workers who would be on strike, not just a few of the most progressive workers in the union with whom we worked on a day-to-day basis.

At the time, CEDRA had, alongside its primary objective of organising with workers at the grassroots level, two working groups – socialist feminist and ecosocialist. Until then, the groups had operated at the level of theory and manifesto writing. With the socialist feminist working group, we were trying to work out how best to implement this perspective in a way that would be meaningful to the workers and they would consider it as their own.

We worked with the union from its very beginning: building a democratic structure, sharing knowledge, organising on the ground and working with the workers at the grassroots level with what were, at first, service-based demands. All the while we were working on the principle of co-research: informing ourselves about the situation – the technical and, therefore, the political composition of retail workers; organising through a mutual relationship of comradeship, politicisation through continuous contact, democratic forms of decision-making, situating their problems and demands within the wider relationship between labour and capital. This is the basis from which it was possible for us to have the trust and willingness of the Red TUŠ committee members and other workers from the union to meet with us and discuss their conditions of labour at the workplace and the situation in their households.

The feminist co-research questionnaire sought to apply the effects of economic mobilisations, trade union struggles, to broader political work. The aim of the co-research was to raise awareness of the issue of exploitation by capital in the context of the production process in the workplace and to link this to the question of the reproductive process in the context of women's oppression under capitalism. Retail workers are mostly women, who are usually tasked with privately relegated reproductive labour in the households before and after their shifts, where they work as reproducers in the private sector.

We met with the committee members of Red TUŠ individually, with three long-term aims: 1. to politicise and raise awareness of the interconnectedness of capitalist production and workers' reproduction at home; 2. to establish a Committee for Common Good inside the TUŠ union, which would deal with the questions of reproductive labour and patriarchy; 3. to familiarise the interviewees with CEDRA and invite them to become part of our organisation.

The main method of feminist co-research is the interview. We formed a questionnaire and divided it into two parts:

(1) In the first part of the interview we ask the workers about their relations at the workplace. The aim of this part of the interview is to acknowledge the difference between two concepts - collegiality and class solidarity. *Collegiality* is what we have called the relationship of mutual help and cooperation between workers that benefits capital. For example, workers helping each other at work and working on tasks that go beyond their obligations (to help coworkers who can't keep up), thus speeding up their own pace or intensity of work; skipping sick days and popping pills (so as not to add a bigger workload to their coworkers); accepting transfers to distant offices (to help coworkers when there are no staff), etc. All these actions, which are perceived by workers as collegiality, allow capital to intensify work or operate at the lowest possible level of employment and increase the rate of exploitation, which in turn allows for higher profits. The aim

of the first part of the interview is to come to an understanding, together with the workers, of how capital benefits from relations of collegiality. The first part, therefore, ends with a discussion of class solidarity, a form of mutual support and cooperation established by the workers during the mobilisation in the context of the trade union struggle, which - unlike collegiality - is autonomous in relation to capital. This is achieved by referring to the moment of resistance, i.e. when the workers came together to resist capital, which happened during the mobilisation and the preparations for the strike.

The structured questionnaire followed the principles of co-research: informing, politicising and organising in a dialogical conversation that puts knowledge on the side of the workers. The interviewer asks the questions which are posed in a way that leads to a specific insight. For example, in the first part of the interview, one of the questions concerns the intensity of labour:
2. iii. What drives you to work at the given level of intensity? Why don't you slow down, make work easier for yourself?

  a. Is it possible to get all the work done if you worked at a slower pace?
  (What happens if you don't complete all the work you were supposed to?)

The instructions in brackets are intended to guide the interviewer towards the goal of moving from an individualist understanding of one's own position towards a materialist viewpoint. The objective is, therefore, not only to gather information about the organisation of labour but also to connect the workers' individual experiences into a class-based perspective. With the question above (2 iii.), we want to come to the conclusion that working at a high intensity of labour is not primarily connected to a person's character or "nature", but the organisation of labour process that forces the workers to work at the highest possible level of intensity since that entails higher profits for the company. Our interviewee answers:

  S: [...] I would say it's my own fault too, because I'm that kind of person, I'm a workaholic, I can't help it, really, [...]
  C: Mhm.
  S: [...] there weren't that many customers, no. But here I got into that "drill" again. I'm just like that by nature, I just can't walk slowly. I mean, yeah, it's in my interest to do more than what you're asked to do. I don't know. We are different, yes.
  C: So that's primarily why you work so hard, would you say?

S: Yeah.

C: That it basically only has to do with you? Mhm. But would you say that it's possible to do all this work at all if you worked slower, let's say?

S: No, it's not possible. I don't know, there are things, I don't know, we have a lot of sick leaves and so, there's really only few of us [...]. I don't know, it forces you, if you're that kind of person, I don't know, go crazy literally at work because you can't do it, it's not working. It's not. So yeah, you get to a state of burnout, I believe that. I've been here for 5 months and yeah, you get [burnout], so it's no wonder girls go, no. Because they can go, because they need to, because the body can't bear it.

(March 2023)

(2) In the second part of the interview, we talk about relations in the household, where we discuss the work they do at home, and again, we come back to the benefits that this brings to capital. That is, we talk about the unpaid reproductive labour they do within the household, which is otherwise ideologically understood as a labour of love. In doing so, we first draw their attention to the benefits that capital derives from unpaid reproductive labour. By analogy with the first part, here we draw their attention to the way in which capital benefits from their relations within the family – from the needs and desires of their close ones. Secondly, we discuss with them possible forms of resistance and class solidarity related to the question of the socialisation of reproductive labour. That is to say, we talk to them about socialisation in general: public canteens, laundries, retirement homes, kindergartens and the problem of care in general. In short, together with the workers, we have come up with demands for collective satisfaction of needs - demands for public canteens, accessible old people's homes, kindergartens, etc.

The example below shows Sanchez's perspective shifting from a position of (only) interpersonal gain of her unpaid reproductive labour for her husband towards an interconnected understanding of work and household spheres, where capital benefits from externalising the costs of reproduction.

1. h. Do you think that anyone benefits from the care and household work you do at home? *(With this question, we move on to the broader issue of the relationship between labour and capital; we are interested in 1) the interpretation of workers, if they have one, but at the same time 2) it is necessary to intervene in order to get to the issue of business being performed at the lowest possible expense for the*

workforce, which is at the expense of the free time of workers, the environment, etc., and to relate to the fact that capital 3) benefits from interconnections, care for loved ones.)

S: Yes, of course they benefit.

P: Who benefits from all of us women doing it at home? We clean, we cook, we feed the children, we take care of the children...

C: But we take it for granted that we do it ...

S: [laughs]

P: My husband profits a little bit too, of course, and the men have a little bit too, definitely. Does anyone else?

S: Yes, thank you for saying that out loud.

P: But does anyone else?

S: So that this isn't silly ...

P: It won't be silly, you just say it.

S: Everyone, no ... The country ... If we do it, if someone does it for us ...

P: Yes.

C: Even Tuš at the end, right? To come to work the next day sorted, all that, and Tuš has nothing to do with it.

S: Of course ...

P: Do you think the capitalists benefit from everyone doing it at home and then coming back another day?

S: That's true, yes ... And that I come back the next day fit, tidy, neat, polished, clean.

C: Yeah, and you have the energy to do it.

S: Yes, of course, exactly. Well done.

C: To be there [at the workplace], to exhaust yourself, to come home, to ...

S: ... I reset so I can come back another day.

P: You feed your child, you feed your husband, so he goes to work.

S: So that he is fed, clean. Yes, really ...

C: You are also preparing the child to continue the same way one day.

S: Yes, into that [ideology]. We are super women. To think about everything that we do, crazy. When someone confronts you like that ... Because you're in it all the time, you don't even look into it.

C: It works well if it's like that.

S: Because it's common sense for you and you do everything routinely.

(March 2023)

The questionnaire turned out to be a meaningful basis for raising awareness on the issues of unpaid reproductive labour and the lack of public services that are in the interest of the working class. To not keep it at the point of raising awareness, a more stable and permanent structure that would allow for continuous work and material changes seemed necessary, therefore, the Committee for Common Good was established. On the issue of organisation of the working process, we have managed to organise a slowdown in some of the shops and a symbolic statement to no longer work above the workers' capacities at others, under the slogan "I won't work for three workers!". On broader social issues that go beyond the workplace, the Committee is more or less stagnant at the moment, only being revived for, for example, the 8th of March and other symbolic political statements. CEDRA's recent re-activation in the areas of health and care work might make it possible for the Committee to start forming material demands and connect with other unions across sectors and other progressive organisations. Our feminist co-research interviews are continuing and have proven to be a useful entry point into CEDRA. The interview is one of CEDRA's first attempts to open a broader social (and socialist) perspective with the workers as a structured and comprehensive intervention that goes beyond short responses to current political events or spontaneous conversation add-ins.

Conclusion: Breaking with formal divisions

The feminist co-research outlined here is not the first systematic workers´ inquiry undertaken by CEDRA. For example, in 2020 and 2021 we conducted an extensive inquiry with Lidl workers that focused on the working conditions in general and workplace injuries in particular. The feminist co-research was the first project explicitly aimed at opening-up space for conversations about social and political issues that go beyond the immediate production process, addressing leisure time, reproductive labour, and public healthcare and education systems.

We are currently considering the potential of co-research to address migrant labour. In retail, we are observing a growing prevalence of precarious employment (migrant work, outsourcing, agency work and the special form of agency work for students - student jobs). Similar to the feminist co-research conducted with mostly female workers in retail, who experience the dual burden of low-paid, back-breaking labor at the workplace and reproductive labour in their own households as a result of increasing inaccessibility of public services, the political character of capitalist exploitation is particularly evident in workplaces that rely on migrant workers. This is because employers manage both the working conditions and legality of migrant workers' stay/residence in the European union.

Just as we worked to challenge the division between productive and reproductive work with the feminist co-research, our political goal with further co-research projects is breaking with the formal divisions between permanent and temporary employment, directly employed and outsourced workers, citizens and migrants, which workplace organising often spontaneously follows, and highlight that although concrete forms of exploitation vary, the struggle is one.

The whole questionnaire can be found on the Notes from Below website.

When Workers Take Control: The Occupation of Harland and Wolff

Joe Passmore

In 2019, after years of mismanagement, the shipbuilding company Harland and Wolff went into administration. With the threat of a corporate takeover refusing to guarantee continued employment, and facing mass redundancies, the unionised workforce at the company's historic Belfast shipyard occupied their workplace. For nine weeks, workers demanded the re-nationalisation of their industry, a transition to green production, and improved employment security. Below, NFB talks with Joe Passmore, a steelworker and senior shop-steward at Harland and Wolff who played a central organising role in coordinating the occupation.

Could you introduce Harland and Wolff's history: who are the company and how long have they operated?

Harland and Wolff (H&W) was formed in 1862. At the time there were two shipyards in Belfast, and by the beginning of the twentieth century, H&W was probably the biggest shipyard in the world. We had up to 35,000 people working there, running out two or three ships each year: which is incredible when we think of how long it takes to build a ship nowadays. Health and safety wasn't a big thing in the past, and I don't think it was in any ship-building company. Fatalities were taken as normal. For every ship launched there were fatalities. It's an awful way to be. There was a human cost to every ship. There was also a hierarchy then, when working people were treated with disdain. For bosses – right up until when I started in the late 1970s – you were there to do a job, and they would have just sacked you at the drop of a hat if you didn't tow the line. So it probably wasn't a good place to work then, like most industries of the time.

In the Titanic-era (the ship was built between 1909-12), everyone looked at the technology we were using. We led the world. Our techniques were way ahead of everyone else. That continued, after a slight lull following the First World War, and into the Second World War, when so many different warships were coming through Belfast. This made it a prime target for the Luftwaffe, and the scars are still there from that, throughout greater Belfast, particularly east Belfast, because it got pounded. It was because they knew the capacity of H&W and what we could do. So the fame has always been there. It's a famous brand, and it's famous because historically we laid the foundations for so many innovations. And we're still at that, breaking moulds and striving ahead with things.

What was your job exactly? What did it involve?

I started as a steelworker, at sixteen, in 1979. There were 15,000 people working there. The whole of Queen's Island was H&W's. We had our own bus service, our own medical centre - which we needed badly, because there were a lot of injuries. It was a real hive. The craftsmen and the people, with the knowledge and skills that were there, it was absolutely incredible. I started working with oxy-acetylene cutting machines, cutting through steel-plate. You had to have a steady hand, and you had to make sure you wore the equipment or else you'd blind yourself. I learned how to caulk (the equivalent of modern riveting). You get a chisel, and use it like a mini kango hammer, and you gouge metal. Hard work, and sore if you don't do it right. You'd come home with a sore arm every day doing it. And it was loud and deafening. It caused a lot of people to go deaf. Many people had white-finger, caused by constant vibration. It wasn't easy, but I was an expert by the end of it. Unfortunately, or perhaps fortunately, after only doing it for a few years, it became illegal.

My main job was burning. I was lucky enough to get introduced to the huge burning machines which cut massive steel plates. You don't learn fast. An old hand taught me, showing me things no one else could do. He'd made up his own tools, creating special applications for semi-automatic machines. He taught me how to make them, how to strip these machines down and rebuild them. I then progressed onto all kinds of gas-cutting machines, and plasma machines. You learned the basics in training centres, but you learn the secrets outside the training centre. You learn specialities. And you don't even know you're learning them, until one day someone comes along and you're the only person they can come to cause you're the only person who knows how to do it.

I think industry has lost that everywhere. Unfortunately, over the last few decades they've stopped doing apprenticeships. There's a boom and bust cycle that takes place within ship-building: we bring people in, the work dries up, then we have all these skilled workers with nothing to do, so they leave and we don't get them back. There are skills we'll never get back, like heat lining, the shaping of plates through heat. These are things needed in modern-day shipbuilding, but we don't have anyone left who can do it. Some people my age learned some of those skills, but not enough to retain it all. So, particularly with what's coming at H&W, we're probably gonna have to bring people from outside to teach us the skills we used to teach to the world.

What is the history of worker organising and trade-unionism at H&W?

When I came in 1979, I went to the convenor's office. He gave me a union card and got me to sign a form, and I didn't do an interview or anything like that, and he said, 'okay, you start next Monday.' That was it. That was the strength of the union then, and the company just accepted that. They feared trade-unions then. Our terms and conditions were, by that point, becoming among the best in the industry. Unions weren't held back by current legislation. If a disagreement was coming, they knew unions had the strength and the wit to pull everyone out. The company sometimes used that to their own advantage. There were mind games. And I'm not saying unions didn't get complacent. In various instances, including in my own, we found that when we relied so much on the union and they had the power to do something, they didn't do it.

But the strength was there. There was nothing to stop them. I was involved in so many strikes over the years, strikes that could be called at the drop of a hat. People walked out over things, sometimes politically motivated, sometimes not, sometimes orchestrated by the company. For example, I recently heard about 'the orange juice strike' at H&W. The company provided orange juice and a cooling-off area for welders working on pipes, because the heat was intense. They came along one day and said: we're taking away your orange juice, we're taking down that cooling-off tent. So everyone walked out. For every day of strike-action, the company was granted an extra week to fulfil its contract. So, it works both ways: it shows the strength of the union, but sometimes unions can be used.

In 2000, I got paid off. There were lots of redundancies around then. I had a back injury, from working on those machines, and lifting heavy objects. I had to be operated on, and it took about four months before I was permitted to go back to work. I returned around May 2000, and one month later pay-offs came out and they told me: 'you're going'. My shop steward initially supported me, but when we met with the personnel manager, he just sat with his head down. I was heart-broken. I'd been there 20 years, and I was about to go. I didn't know what would happen after that.

So you lose faith in unions. I know I did. I was out of there for almost thirteen years, I had some really good jobs, but I never joined a union. Because I felt let down and I thought - how can you depend on people like that? I was in GMB then. If there is such a thing as demarcation of trades, within unions, it existed then: we were told every steelworker, welder, has to be in GMB. Everyone else was in Unite. When I later returned to H&W, it took me a while to get my head straight. I ultimately thought: 'I'm gonna have to join a union'. But I decided never will I join the GMB. So that's when I joined Unite. And, interestingly, when I joined Unite and I started working for people, initially as a Health and Safety rep, I managed to bring half the steelworkers and welders along, and they left GMB. So we broke that monopoly.

Historically, trade-unions were slightly different in this country. The difficulty with Northern Ireland is that unions could get hijacked by paramilitary forces. I know that was the case in H&W. Not for one minute would I ever tell anyone that H&W was not sectarian: when I was there, in the 1970s, it was. Catholic workers were 'tolerated', but they were pointed at whenever things went wrong, and that was encouraged by some shop-stewards because some were paramilitaries themselves. You could have said that about this whole country then. People in power like that tended to go that way. It was difficult, and H&W was a microcosm of this whole country. People who shouldn't have been in power got into power, and held influence when they didn't. You can understand why a lot of people weren't going to work in the shipyards then: because of fear. Fear of what can happen. And that was union-driven.

Were there instances of solidarity between Catholic and Protestant workers?

I was there when one murder took place. A worker, Maurice O'Kane, was shot dead in the bottom of a ship's tank. It was a Loyalist-sanctioned killing. Police were involved, I know the nurse who came down to see to the guy afterwards. It was just blatant: someone brought a gun into the yard, if it wasn't already there, and shot a guy in the back of his head because he was Catholic. I remember the next day we held a mass meeting and a minute's silence, and it was speech after speech, coming out and saying 'we're meant to be one shipyard, one people, it doesn't matter what your opinion is but this just destroys us and our community.' With that hatred going on, and when it gets to that extreme, so many people put the brakes on, and say that's enough. This is about us, workers, and it should never cross that line again. It quietened down after that, there was a step change. But those old prejudices crept in again from time to time.

I saw workers' unity when the company reneged on a pay agreement. A ship was due to come out of the dock. The unions didn't even lead this, this was workers. They realised that if they want to get a ship out of the dry dock, you're gonna have to move the dock-gate and float it out to the commissioning quay, and there's money attached to that. Just a few forklift drivers to start with, and then everyone else just gathered on the dock gate and said 'you're not moving it while we're standing here. Where's our pay rise?' The company gave in because they were gonna lose a fortune by not taking this ship out. That was solidarity at its finest.

What was the background to the 2019 occupation?

I came back to H&W in 2013. After a few years, the opportunity came up for a safety rep, and I put my name forward. I took it seriously, and people had faith in me. After six months, I got involved in pay negotiations. I realised there was a no-strike clause in a pay agreement. I said I'm not happy with this, I'm not putting my signature near this until it's removed. GMB, I have to say, turned on me. 'We've been waiting on this raise for a long time, and you've blocked it', they said. 'Take it out and we don't have a problem', I said. Susan, our regional secretary, backed me to the hilt, telling all the Unite people in H&W what was going on. They ultimately removed it. I was able to come back and say 'fine, that's okay.' So I gained a lot of respect out of that.

At that time, H&W was put up for sale. A Newry firm, MJM, came saying they were going to bring cruise ships into H&W. We were suspicious because this company had cruise ships in before. They used their own workers: foreign workers, brought in from overseas, and they weren't allowed off the ships. We know they were on very poor wages. Our view was that this was providing absolutely nothing to the local economy. It's not doing H&W or our community any favours. Now these are the people wanting to buy us and bring in their own cruise ships, and we thought: are our jobs in danger here? Is this what they're thinking? To get rid of us and ship foreign workers in and treat them like slaves? Cause that's what it looks like.

Anyway, they played the game. They should have made an offer by June. In the middle of July they said - look, we've dropped our asking price from 7m to 2m, and we're not bringing the original workforce across. So we got politicians and various agencies round the table to resolve this. By this stage the company was heading for administration. The politicians all had their own agendas. These involved 'okay mate, we'll make sure you get proper advice for your new jobs', things like that. That's not what we wanted to hear. We were never going to accept redundancies. We wanted to fight redundancies. We wanted a change in Harland.

How did the occupation emerge as a strategic action, and how was it coordinated?

When MJM let us down, we decided - okay, we're gonna do something about this. Now, it wasn't difficult, because everyone had seen it heading in this direction, and we'd been having regular meetings about the situation. I have close friends in Ford Visteon, who, ten years before this, had occupied their plant in west Belfast over pensions. I'd been hearing their stories about their situation and what they did. So this was lodged in my head. And of course Susan said to me - did you hear what happened on the Clyde in the 1970s? So she egged me on, but I'd already had the thought because of my friends. And I thought that was the way to go. It was that bloody-mindedness, thinking - what have we got to lose? Why should we just give up and put our heads down?

We started organising what we called the original 'cobra committee', like the government's COBRA committee: a council of war. This involved electricians who looked after the electronic gates, joiners, and riggers and heavy machinery operators: just everyone who had any influence. We set out an agenda at each of these meetings – which we had in front of everyone at our canteen, so everyone could see what was going on, so no workers were isolated. We said - 'here's what your job is going to be', and we listed what had to be done, because at that stage we knew that if we were going to take a stand, we had to make the preparations. If this goes to the wall, we're gonna be ready for it.

So, for example, the heavy machinery operators. To take control of the place, we needed to have access to an entrance that we controlled. So all the heavy machinery operators were prepped to move concrete blocks near to the other entrance gates, days before anything happened. We got our painters and joinery people to create the biggest banner they possibly could to hang over our giant cranes – to let Belfast know that we were taking a stand. We had electricians putting small fixes into electronic turnstiles, so that we could access them, and so we couldn't be locked out. We had secret back doors into the yard, as we got our joinery department to change the locks. We talked this through and worked out this agenda in front of everyone. We worked out how we would treat the press. We worked out provisions: who was going to look after and manage these.

We had staff on notice to make sure people were there around the clock. We used all the skills available to us to make it effective.

I'd had meetings with Susan in the Clayton Hotel in Belfast. It was like cloak and dagger stuff. We decided to occupy on the Monday ahead of administration. Our idea was that if we wait until administration, we'd be on the outside looking in. The power had to be in the hands of the workers: if we hit before administration, and we control it, then we're on the inside looking out.

So, that Monday lunchtime, I went to the CEO, and said: 'can you tell me if MJM have changed their mind and are going to bring over our workforce? Or do we have another bidder?' He said no, we don't have any of that, and we'd be going into administration the Thursday of that week. So I told him we've no other choice - 'from a union perspective, we're going to take things into our own hands.' I left and went straight to our canteen. I had already called a mass meeting, we had staff, absolutely everyone, senior management and all. I said - 'look, I'm not about to give this shipyard up easily, and I don't think any of you are either. I wanna take a stand. You know what that stand involves. I'm ready to do it, are you ready to do it?' The place erupted and everyone walked to the gate.

Right from the start, we told the security guys - you can do your checks, your business, whatever you're going to do. But we control this site, and we say who comes in and who doesn't. We more or less policed it. Our original thought was to barricade the gate. We don't want any vultures coming in to asset-strip the yard. We created a big list of people who were not getting in. But we also thought - you know what, we don't want to make this place locked down. When anything promising and serious came along, we arranged a tour around the yard ourselves to show our facilities.

The occupation hit headlines. It gathered momentum. We got administration pushed back. And we had objectives: to keep the vultures out, pressurise the government, and 're-nationalise.'

There were also demands around green re-tooling?

One of the last projects we worked on prior to the occupation involved 'jackets': the base for off-shore wind turbines. We previously worked on oil-drilling platforms. Huge trenches, huge holes, were dug in the seabed to anchor these. It was someone from H&W who came up and said, 'if you put a cup upside down in water you can create suction, if you get this down there and blow all the air out of that, it's going to stick to anything.' So we did that, we invented that, we got it so that you put these huge suction cups down to the seabed, and then blow all the air from the outside-in. You're doing nothing but using the earth and suction to hold it down. They're all over the world now. We did them first.

There is nothing stopping us from doing this again, these innovations based on shipbuilding. It wasn't all about ships, about oil, it was about how to make it greener, how to make it work better. And we were doing that. We took what existed there and we changed it for a better environment. To have those facilities to be able to do that, to have those huge cranes, to have that massive dry dock (the biggest in Europe), and not use it for that? That is ludicrous. Such a waste. That's why we had colleagues with a similar outlook from around the world who see the value of H&W and what we can do, and what we can change. So during the occupation green re-tooling was an aspiration, but we'd already laid the foundation for that aspiration to become serious.

What did day-to-day organising inside the occupation look like? What was your strategy?

After that first day of the occupation, we saw the success we had across the news, and that the occupation was having an impact internationally. We created a new cobra committee to discuss strategy. We met every day to plan what we were going to do next. One idea was to get ourselves on the news every single night. Let's get everyone talking. We used social media to extremes. I was coming out with messages on social media that were reaching 35,000 people every day.

We marched to Stormont. There was an incident there with an Irish-language campaign group. We'd been there, alongside different groups, to protest Boris Johnson's visit. There were all these shipyard workers, and in front of us there were all these Irish language activists who did not want to be politically associated, who had their own thing, and didn't want political parties getting involved. I went up to one of the girls there, and I asked: 'what's "save our shipyard" in Irish?' She told me, and I spoke to the rest of the guys, and then we started chanting and shouting 'save our shipyard' in Irish [sábháil ár longchlós!].

A BBC journalist spoke to me after and asked, 'have I just seen a change in the politics of Northern Ireland?' Because we were still perceived by some as some kind of loyalist bastion.[44] So that was momentous, because it moved from people thinking 'there's those Protestants making a load of noise again', to 'Jesus, they're fighting for workers' rights here'. Chanting in Irish was a really powerful, unifying moment, where we had the whole community behind us. If you look at the news from that night, it wasn't even about Boris Johnson. It was about shipyard workers and it was about the Irish language.

We also had Belfast Pride in the middle of the occupation. We had a fleet of flags brought down by Unite, including Pride flags, and a picture of me tying the Pride flag to our gate went everywhere. The Pride march had a banner leading it with 'support Harland and Wolff': because we made one small action with that flag.

What did the occupation achieve, and what does H&W's future look like?

It was tense right up to the end. We'd been there for nine weeks. What we did in the end was make that shipyard work again. We ultimately got another buyer, who agreed to bring across the workforce. This provided five years' work that we would not have had if H&W were to close.

Now, ultimately, it was the wrong people we got in. The business model put us in crisis again. They tried to build a corporation from the shipyard, when the shipyard had to grow first. The news about administration in 2024: it's the PLC. Millions wasted on a whole corporate entity within London, which the four yards are now dealing with. A lot of the company's debt came from there, from tiers upon tiers of ridiculous job titles, and directors of this and that. We even had a director of vending machines. That's how ludicrous it got. No matter how much I hate it, we have been open five years, we have expanded the workforce, and I am grateful for that.

We're currently at a stage now where we're on the verge of getting taken over by a Spanish yard. They're state-owned, so have avoided much of that boom and bust cycle where we fell behind. They've embraced modern technology that we let go by us.

I think it will be a smooth transition. If we'd gotten bad news recently, then we would have blockaded those gates again. I would have had the keys out for back-doorways into the yard. I would have had everyone there down at that gate. We will always have a way in. And when one door closes we will always find another one.

---

44   When I went back to work in H&W in 2013, it was a changed place. No one asked what religion you were anymore. It just wasn't a question.